From J
to City Hall

Your Resume Can Change

Shamann Walton

I would like to dedicate this book and the chapters my life will continue to write to Philmore Graham. The man who interjected on the story I was writing and not only showed me it was possible to change the script but taught me by example and exposure the chapters I could write if I really wanted to.

About the Author

Shamann Walton is currently the President of the San Francisco Board of Supervisors. Born in San Francisco, he lived in public housing at an early age in both the Bayview Hunters Point and Potrero Hill neighborhoods. At the age of 11, he moved to Vallejo, CA, with his mother, where he endured many challenges, from losing childhood friends to witnessing violence (domestic and community), teen parenting, and incarceration. As an accomplished and experienced community leader, Shamann has dedicated his life to improving the lives of others and changing these realities in our community.

Shamann is the proud father of his children: Monique, Malcolm, Damani, and Dominic (all adults now). He is extremely happy to be the grandparents of Emari, Symone, Emiyah and Damani Jr. and lives in San Francisco's Bayview Hunters Point community with his wife, Mesha. Shamann has a bachelor's degree in Political Science from Morris Brown College and a master's degree in Public Administration from San Francisco State University.

Shamann continues to work in his community and fight for policies that work to achieve equity, address racial bias, and provide opportunities for those who need us the most. He is on a quest to guarantee, like his mentor Philmore Graham, that all young people can succeed given the opportunity and information needed for success.

Table of Contents

Foreword

When Shamann first mentioned his book, I thought it both fitting for him and freeing for others that he would "stand" and speak to the truth of the road he has traveled, encouraging fathers and sons to begin or continue the conversation on who they are and the possibilities that exist beyond the frame of the world we live in as they read these pages. But, really, his message crosses gender lines, and for anyone who reads his story, it serves as a potent reminder that at any given time in life, we can change the script our life is writing if we really want to and use our past as our footstool.

We, at times, give in to the temptation to hide parts of our background and our perceived skeletons, functioning in a world of pretense while carrying around boxes of insecurities and shame. Shamann's bold belief in transparency equips him with the audacious faith to open the door to all areas of his life and tell it like it is. He has in no way ever glamorized his past, but rather sees the value in sharing the details to inspire someone else that they too can overcome challenges and not be defined by them. It matters not from where we begin; it matters mostly that against all odds – we do. The content on these pages will inspire at least one person, who will at the least inspire one more to be free. Isn't that what we all really want - to experience what it feels like to live completely free? To feel courageous enough to say that this is unapologetically my past or where I am presently, but I know there's a better version of myself that I was sent here to deliver on, and I am simply a work in progress. It is in these simple acts of bold transparency that we are able to pull the cover from over what we consider our darkest moments and evolve more fully into who we really really are. Each new moment brings with it a chance to begin again, yet the gift of a clean slate that it brings with it is at times missed by our perspective. After all, isn't our acquired knowledge based on trial and error to some degree, and the present and future our playground to write it as we think possible for ourselves? Not everyone realizes it as such, and those moments when we don't turn the corner into the new, we allow our past to keep us stuck in what has been, who we were, and the belief that the extent of our future reach is determined solely by things that only matter because we have carved out a space for them in the crevices of our thoughts. I think I would have found myself stuck "there" a few times if it was not for the patient voice I would hear after sharing the details pertaining to less-than-stellar moments. What are you going to do now? And I often did not have my next steps thought through immediately, and that was okay. What was not given room to grow in our conversation was time spent wondering what someone else would think or say about me. Judgment, he has always reminded me, is the powerful space we allot to others for them to 'dictate' at any given moment what we do and where we go from that point. When we accept what has been and any role we played, pray about it and make forgiveness of self and others our focus, what anyone else thinks has no power and does not enter our sphere. "Be honest with yourself and remain steadily moving forward, always."

So often we meet people and admire them for who we see before us without ever really knowing the distance they traveled and the miles they overcame to arrive at this point. In these chapters, you will be walked through the life of a child who some may have thought would not be here today, but here he is, the man who fought against the hold of his past to experience a life he eventually accepted would be his.

It comes as no surprise that the person whose ear of trust I've often been most transparent with, encourages me then as he does now to be so resilient in my chase and committed to my goals that I may manage to avoid the trap of trying to master the trivial. I, at times, have become so distracted by an outcome I was not expecting that I would hold myself still in my tracks trying to decipher how it went South, why what happened occurred, and revisit my thinking that led me there. When I was younger, rolling with the punches was not one of my greatest strengths, and looking back, I now marvel at how kind life is that it would cause my paths to overlap with someone who would play a critical role in helping me to grow in this area. While being the ear, Shamann would balance the role of listener and pity party interrupter. "No, you have not failed, nor are you... We all stumble, and no one is perfect. But are you learning and growing?" he would ask. My list of teachable moments is endless, but for every case of poor judgment, he has been there to remind me not to get buried in life. The layers of who we are makes us 'rich' in this world, and only those who are able to share their entire life story with whomever their chosen audience have a chance to fully experience the freedom of self-acceptance. To live in a world held captive by self-imposed limitations, I equate with living as a prisoner and never knowing we were indeed free all along. These encounters do make me more cognizant of the respective roles people play in our lives and how valuable your corner team is to personal growth and overall progress.

The mere fact that we met often brings to mind the kindness of people. A man claims a young boy as his own, and believes so deeply in his better self that he sacrificed time, effort, and resources to grant him the gift of exposure. If it was not for Mr. Graham, who knows if I would have met Shamann, and I often ponder whose life I will impact to that magnitude. How will my time here make another person's life better? Which village have I created, and how are the villagers better today than when we first met? I have only been in his presence twice, but the ripple effect his actions caused to flow downstream has been a significant reminder that life is bigger than my personal ambitions and fulfilling my dreams. The true weight of our presence is in the footprints blazing their own trail because we took the time to impact their lives. In my quiet time, I find myself in thought on whose dreams I'm helping to come to fruition, and whose not yet realized potential am I helping to shine a light on? When I think myself too busy or not best positioned to reach back and speak life into our young dreamers or peer sleepers, another silent message that I grabbed from years of hearing Shamann talk about Mr. Graham whispers, "you don't need a title or to have achieved a certain level of success to reach back and help someone, you really just have to be willing and present." How much good would we really do, if we started functioning in a barrier-less world where I thought outside of "just mine," and you thought beyond "just yours," and we all just wanted everyone to make it?

It was our freshman week - over 20 years ago when Shamann and I first met. He has seen me through some of my worst days and most confusing times, celebrated with me during some of the better days, and been a part of some of my favorite moments. To label this "friendship" feels restrictive. I consider this my breathing space. Where I can think out loud, make unfiltered statements and ask any question that comes to mind. There are no requirements, and the measurement of the influence is not in the frequency of conversation but rather in the consistently free-flowing energy between people who genuinely mean each other well. I have at times heard others say that their best friendships are with those they share the most similarities. In my case, I would have to say my most powerful relationships are fueled by exchanges that foster growth and serve as conscience mirrors when needed.

I vividly remember post-undergrad life when we lived in the same city and would go for our lunch outings to T. G. I. Fridays. Our talks would cover so much ground on any range of topics. Whether it was me talking about relationships, exchanging thoughts on how our futures would be written, or asking endless hypothetical questions, Shamann would be there patiently answering and playing devil's advocate when nudged to do so. But always direct/truthful. It's as if every question was being answered so as to be sure whatever was being spoken; if that was the last thing that was ever said, it would be a nugget of wisdom powerful enough to remain in my thoughts. This I have found to be both safe and treasured. What he says he means and the value he places on the bond of friendship and confidentiality makes him well-liked and well-known. I cannot remember a time when I picked up the phone or sent him an email and felt the need to preface what I was about to say with "please don't tell anyone" or "can this stay between us". He hears my most random thoughts that are often met with his direct responses, which he knows will be followed by more questions than what the average person would ask. Yet there is not a time when he didn't answer each one or question a thought I had if necessary. When I read through the pages of this book, that's the person I see. A man grounded in honesty, giving no thought to what others may think because he remains so focused on a bigger vision of life, which is to do what he can to positively impact a few lives with his transparency. We sometimes just need a reminder that someone else has been where we are, and change indeed is possible. My hope for everyone is that they have at least one person in their corner who they can share their most embarrassing and personal stories with and not feel the sting of judgment but rather the confidence of truth and comfortable vulnerability.

He has asked me, and if you met, he may ask you, "What is it that you want for yourself? And what are you doing to make it happen?" I must forewarn you, when you do meet, should you decide to preface your response to that question with a "But" as you begin to explain all the reasons why something will not or has not happened for you, please know that he may give you the same three-word response, in the same kind tone he has given me previously "Those are excuses." So get ready to map out a strategy. Life really is a business, and it requires balancing all areas in the book of living. "Free time", he has told me, "simply does not exist." We are paying for it in how we spend each minute that we are given. Living with a sense of purpose, regardless of how large or small our platform, is to live with the notion that someone paid the price for you to stand on their shoulders, and someone will need to stand on yours. But where will it take them? How will they be elevated to another level because you were born?

Who would have known when this book started to be written that we were moving towards a time of increased crime, senseless killings, and a steady decline in the percentage of young males enrolling in universities and trade programs. As each chapter was written, I could not help but notice the correlation between the life he transitioned from and how critical it is that he now share his experiences with youth, fathers, and families who may know no other way than their immediate environment or need to be refueled to believe that they really have a way out to a higher road if desired. The village, his story reminds us, is one of the most critical tools in executing change. You don't have to be a parent to make a child's life better, nor do you have to give birth to a baby to be their responsible parent figure. Every child won't have the desire or genuine interest to pursue a university degree, but what are their gifts and their talents, and how can we help them to maximize their gifts and talents?

I was honored to be asked to write the foreword for this book, and I hope as you turn each page, you will be inspired to share your own story with someone who may need to see what hope looks like and know that change though difficult is possible; that the eyes that connect with these words will be reminded that their present circumstances, whatever they may be, are not the extent of who they are. Regardless of where we find ourselves in life, there is always a fork in the road where we need to choose to either abort change and stay the same or take the path less traveled and get comfortable with the unknown on nothing more than a desire to see what it is that life has for me. If the pages had an audible voice, I could hear them asking, "Do you believe that you can be more than you are right at this moment, and are you willing to commit to the work needed to get you there?" It is also my hope that the universal village caretakers will increase in numbers and we will return to a time where I am my sisters' and brothers' and their children's keeper. As we know and are often reminded, it takes only one person and sometimes only one encounter to positively impact a life. We want everyone to make it.

– Foreword written by the Co-Author,
Ms. Keisha James

I sit in my room in silence, glancing between the four walls surrounding me. Each wall telling its own story. Each thought creating its own moment of reflection. The daunting challenge of keeping the snapshots of my memory separate becomes unmanageable. My brain caves in, and each roaming thought comes rushing in at the same moment, demanding my immediate attention. But this very familiar place has become too comfortable for me. Juvenile hall had become my home away from home; a place I hated, yet could not resist the temptations that would keep me away. Each visit leaving me vowing to never return, but somehow the memory of my promises quickly fade with the scent of freedom and the curse of choice. I had managed to maintain some consistency, as the reasons for my return usually had one common denominator, with the difference being only a slight twist. This time I was placed in I.S.U. (Intensive Security Unit) because there was a gun involved. So here I am at 16 years old, awaiting trial for an armed robbery charge. My probation officer is here once again, and I have lost count how many times she has stood in my defense. This time she is left deflated from the puzzle of trying to keep me free. But how do you fight for the freedom of another whose actions and thoughts, when left unmonitored, mirrors that of the imprisoned? Bound by poor choices and the deadly cocktail of the resilience and ignorance of a teenager. A better way that constantly reroutes me to the worse way. She is not trying to work with me today. Can you blame her? How many times will we walk down the same road together with me, promising to do better only to continue a cyclical route? This time, if I lose, there is a placement waiting for me. The odds are against me. My future more unpredictable than its ever been. Am I sad? Am I scared? I sure am, but this is not the time to appear weak. The show of emotion would translate into a belief that I am better than my circumstances, that somewhere beneath the surface, I desire another life. I do, but my actions tell a conflicting story, and any change in script I fear breeds uncertainty. I don't know another way. I have to hold it down for myself and for the park.

My daughter is just a baby, and though she needs me, I cannot do anything for her. I am in the eleventh grade and responsible for a human being who I helped to create, but lacking the depth needed to conceptualize the magnitude of the role I need to play. What kind of parent am I? Even at her age though she cannot talk, she can recognize the consistent faces versus someone whose place in her life she cannot quite determine. I am too young to have a child; to add to it, my growing record has set me back even further from the starting line. I think about her daily and cannot help but to ponder on the cycle that our gene pool is on the cusp of repeating. Could I avoid repeating the errs of my mostly absent father, or was this the road I, too, would take? Who will be the one to take care of her and protect her? Who will be the male presence in her life teaching her what she needs to know from a father's standpoint? Clouded by the many questions, I realize that this time it is bigger than just me. I want to do better, but truthfully I don't know how to get there. Who am I? Where do I go from here?

As I walk through the courthouse, I can hear the links from the chains on my feet hitting against the floor. My feet and my arms are restricted with all links to the chains connected around me. We are walking. Walking into a day that is completely out of our control. I see the many stares from the families and people in the building representing freedom. To be on the other side. The ability to walk and move as you please. These basics I crave. My eyes connect with my mother's stare. An expression to this day I have been unable to let go of. On her face, I see disappointment. In her eyes, I see a story of fear and sadness. Hopelessness, if you will. To watch your son drowning in the quicksand of life, each time getting deeper as you are stretched from the sidelines trying to get him out. With each effort, he tries to find his own way but instead failing to find a solid footing. This could not have been her dream for me when she first held me as a baby or as she calculated the sacrifices she so willingly made. She could have opted to not show up today, but here she is. To know what unconditional feels like through maternal love yet struggle with it due to an ongoing battle with the demons of the streets gifts me with a gift I fail to understand time and time again. How can I now make her proud? Is it too late for me?

From Juvenile Hall to City Hall

The year is 1991. My future, if scripted, could be summed up in two words: incarceration and instability. Not too far from what I have come to know, but not the reality I want for myself. Can I change – what does that look like? Do I really have what it takes to lead a completely different lifestyle and make a positive difference? Or will my life be defined by what appears to be my present destiny?

Chapter 1: Grandma

"Goodbye, grandma." I would smile, and she would smile back. "Don't say goodbye, Shamann, say so long. Goodbye is forever." These were the words my grandmother and I would exchange every morning on my way to school. **I was in the 4th grade at the time and heading to school on the city bus as opposed to the school bus that my grandparents believed me to be on. Looking back, this was probably the beginning of my rebellious nature. My thought to seek another route than the one I was instructed to take because that's the route I thought best.**

On the weekends, I would leave to go and stay with my mom, aunt, and my cousins and return on Sunday after church. Now my mom and I did not make it to church every Sunday, but amidst the instabilities in some other areas of my life, church and the development of a spiritual life would be one of few areas where you would find us on the same page. I can't quite explain it, but there was something about being in church that I really enjoyed. It was almost as if it was the calm in the storm. So much so that even though I may not have fully understood the magnitude of being baptized as a young child, at nine years old, I told my mom, it was time for me to take that step. The physical motion of being dipped into water and the laying on of hands caught my attention and quickly vanished as I tried to process everything else happening around me. Seeing guns, drugs, and gangs on a daily basis made the sanctuary seem like a very serene place. Could this holy water really save me? Was this dip going to keep me safe when I ventured down the alley and witnessed a gun aimed to my right? If substance abuse was already not a big enough issue, the times made way for the debut of crack in our community. Ironically, I loved this place. Hunters Point was family. We were a close-knit community, all vying to survive while helping those around us.

In those days, I would get home from school and make an immediate B-line to hang with the other knuckleheads outside. The streets of Hunters Point (affectionately called HP), San Francisco, were ours to roam and claim as we pleased. That truly was through the eyes of children who chose to live as freely as the streets allowed. If you had a fear, HP would quickly bring it to the surface, force you to be an overcomer, or become a victim. It really was that simple. Its tough exterior was only a loose disguise for the even tougher intricacies needed to maneuver through its streets. Violence and crime ran rampant, the evidence of drugs and substance abuse all around. Yet ironically, after the dust settled, the support and comradeship we had for each other made me love this place. How could it be that amongst the very little that we all had and the everyday presence of very little around us, that we would hold tight to some dream of a better day? That a child merely nine years old would be a dope carrier to 3rd Street - the main corridor in Hunters Point and be able to one day tell the story in first person and dream and live a very different life. Everyone from any project will tell you that their neighborhood is the toughest, but I can honestly say that in Hunters Point, you had to be a soldier to make it from day to day. Unfortunately, I wasn't a soldier at the time, but like I said, Hunters Point has a way of fixing things.

When I would hang out in the neighborhood, I would always get beat up by the kids my age, and like everything else, word spread quickly, and I became the moving target. I would run from fights, and at other times I would just stay put and let people hit me. Was I afraid to hit back or too fearful of getting hurt? The rationale I cannot explain, but like any other stage in life, retaliation is forced out only when it gets under your skin enough and becomes unbearable or you want to change the outcome. Whatever the excuse at the time, I was fortunate enough to be living under the same roof as my Uncle Corey – my mother's brother, who is only four years older than I am. He was my childhood hero. In every way, I wanted to be like him. He was popular, always dapper, and his presence unchallenged. Having me as a nephew at the time proved slightly embarrassing for him, and there were times when he would lock me outside and let someone beat me up on our own porch. To his defense, not like he needed one then or now; he recognized my weaknesses and wanted to do his part in preventing me from becoming a 'mama's boy', the potential of which statistics claim are higher with the somewhat limited male presence in my life. With the added pressure from all of his friends, who had little brothers and cousins who were tough and quite good with their hands, he was determined to toughen me up. I would follow him around, emulate his behavior, even going as far as dressing as he did, but my fear of fighting back had a stronger hold on me than my respect for this man (really my peer in my eyes at the time) whom I looked up to. Respect or not, Uncle Corey did not exactly welcome the idea of me being his not-too-distant shadow. Following in his footsteps, but with noticeable gaps in strength of character. As much as my lack of fight annoyed him, the only thing that perturbed him more was that of being thirteen and having me, a nine-year-old at the time, hanging out with him and staying out just as late at parties. I was down with the latest dance moves like the wop and the cabbage patch, learned from observation and practice how to approach girls –those unspoken do's and don'ts. A life-saving lesson was learning not to repeat the things I saw or develop traits of being a snitch. Worse than being a punk was being a tattle tail. In Uncle Corey's eyes, though, they might as well be the same. There were times he would chase me home in an effort to make me leave him alone. I would never test his patience while my fight was still struggling to announce itself.

There comes a point in time in every boy's life when you want to prove yourself to someone you admire. You don't see it that way at the time, but there is always someone you respect enough and hope to one day have that respect reciprocated. One night my need to have that bond with Uncle Corey became stronger than the fear that often kept me sitting open to being punked. I remember this moment like it was yesterday. Its importance still relevant to the different courses our relationship traveled.

My grandparents, uncle, and I were not rich in terms of material wealth but wealthy in love and the memories we shared. We were taught to be comfortable in our own skin – not ashamed that we had to ask our neighbors for sugar or any daily necessities or that our home would have a roach or two. That our house was not surrounded by a white picket fence, but rather that there was always a tomorrow – where in our choosing, we may opt for a better life. We were also taught by Grandma that everyone begins somewhere. Where we go from our starting point is truly dictated by where we focus our compass. Education would be our ticket to where ever we wanted to go. Intelligence gained from the streets and in the classroom would be our survival tools. School was a necessity – no questions asked. And I agreed. There was a certain thrill I got from pushing myself academically beyond the expectations of others. Uncle Corey added one more nugget: sitting back and having life pounce on you is simply unacceptable. Get the grades, but also have the fight. My rules weren't many, and my expectations across the board were made clear early on.

The wind of change had left my mother and I in-between apartments in Fremont and brought me to live with my grandparents for a year while my mother lived with my aunt. Though this living arrangement might in itself strike you as a tad unusual, it gave us a chance to coexist while keeping us off the streets in between our next relocation strategy. We were in need of help, and family pitched in like they always did. While one may try to find the reason or associate the blame for our struggle, I firmly believe we create our own circumstances based on the choices we make, and you would have to know my mother to understand her resilience to do whatever it took to make it to a better place.

One night, my grandmother and I had a long conversation about how well I was doing in school and how convinced she was that I would continue to make the family proud. She had to be the most loving person I knew. After our conversation, I went outside, found my uncle, and told him that I wanted to fight this boy from the neighborhood. Not because he had done something to me, but Grandma's earlier conversation on making the family proud may have somehow fueled me to want to reach this turning point in my relationship with Uncle Corey. His friend went to get his little brother, and we fought at the park on West Point Road. In the beginning, I put a good whipping on this kid, but like every fight, each of us took turns in being the winner. At one point, he got on top of me, and my uncle, probably noticing that I needed another motivation (or just adding a precautionary measure in case wimpy resurfaced), got close enough to tell me that if I reversed it, he would make me a batch of chocolate chip cookies. And so I did. Everybody from West Point was there, and this made my uncle really proud of me; he looked at me a different way that night. However, I went back to my scary stage a few days later when the cousin of the boy I fought wanted to fight me. Even with my newfound confidence, I ran home, proving that sometimes the more things change, the more they stay the same.

It may catch you by surprise, or not, that at nine years old, I was still sleeping with my grandmother periodically. In my eyes, she represented unconditional love. All her grandkids knew they had a special place in her heart. She always took our sides when we were at odds with our parents. Yell at her grandkids, and you were instructed to not come to her funeral. She didn't like it when I slept with her because I was a wild sleeper, and her health, the full extent of which I did not know at the time, was on a steady decline. She taught us all the importance of family and the value of remaining close in spite of what life took us through. Like any other family, ours was divided by the 'haves and the have-nots,' and those on either side remained looped into those on their side of the fence. Hence strangers on our left and right, down the street, and around the corner became our family, much closer than the privileged in our bloodline. This I could not understand but quickly learned to not care. Grandma was rich in a lot of ways, and money had nothing to do with it. Even though we lived in the projects, she had such an aura about her that what we lacked was dulled by her presence and her love. She made us close, and this was actually the case with most of the families in West Point - the street we lived on in Hunters Point.

School ended that year, and so did my time at Grandma's and Grandpa's. I bid the 4th-grade year adieu and was sent off to spend the summer at my father's house. I was all boy and had succeeded at wearing my mother out. Though this was not without some concern on her part due to the bad elements that I would continue to be exposed to while under his care. She took a chance that summer, caught somewhere between a rock and a very hard place. On one end, she wanted us to have a father-son relationship, and on the other end, this was at the risk of spending more time with the very man who was abusive to her.

"Goodbye, grandma," but this time, there was no correction. No response from the woman who taught me more about life in one year than most learn their whole lives. If I had known that when I moved to my father's house, my grandma only had a couple months to live, would I have still gone to a man's house who played no substantial role in my life? Well, not in comparison to Grandma. I had so many roaming thoughts. How long was her stomach being eaten by cancer cells? Why did no one tell me the severity of her illness? And why wasn't I given a chance to visit her and say our goodbyes?

To say that I was being protected from the details of death was an excuse that carried no weight with me. Death was all around me. Whether in the passing away of people in the community or the dying of people who were alive but really dying the slow death of alcoholism, drug addiction, or poverty of mind. I had seen firsthand my mother being abused, seen her drunk, and my father use drugs and the rage that often followed. To not be able to see my grandmother in the hospital and hold her hand or give her a hug, as she had many times done when I needed it, defies my understanding. To come to grips with the fact that when I walked out of her house, that two-bedroom home at 32 WestPoint Road, it would be the last time I saw Grandma alive made me beyond pissed at my mother.

In true fashion, grandma – the youngest of nine children from Rodessa, Louisiana, had the uncanny knack for bringing family together. Her funeral was no different. Filled with the haves and the have-nots was a true testament to who she was and the importance of everyone coming together. I sat at that funeral and cried from beginning to end. Regardless of how important any of the pallbearers and speakers were, death had its way of leveling the playing field. No one more important than the next. In this case, no one was more important than the still body in the casket being carried. Flashbacks of our long talks and jokes came to mind. I cried even more.

Goodbye Grandma. And with that, summer ended, and my mom, her boyfriend James, and I moved from San Francisco to Mountain View, California. Goodbye HP.

Chapter 2: Vallejo

I spent my fifth-grade school year in Mountain View, where I learned to embrace diversity. I was the only black kid in my crew; everyone else was Filipino or white. During this time, I also discovered that girls in Mountain View thought I was cute. The internal fight between doing right and my troubled side continued, as did my academic achievements. Though I was in the GATE (Gifted And Intelligent Program), mischief still had a way of beckoning me from afar. Call it boredom or simply the need to be engaged; during downtime, trouble always found me, or actually, I went in search of it. This marks the time when I began getting suspended from school on a regular basis. I was definitely the kind of child you had to keep busy, or I would have too much time to create my own "busy-ness" to occupy my days. In between school and my paper route, my time in Mountain View was reduced even further by our weekend trips to San Francisco, where I stayed with Uncle Corey and Grandpa or aunties and cousins. During that year, Mom and James were able to save enough money to buy a house in Vallejo, and the summer following, we moved. My new life began, but not without a deeper continuation of my past.

At the time, Vallejo was an undeveloped small city and not really a part of the bay area. Being more of a bedroom community that offered new housing at cheaper costs for first-time homeowners and employment opportunities at the naval base, there was an influx of people moving from San Francisco to Vallejo. Just as we were moving in, Marine World Africa USA (now known as Six Flags Discovery Kingdom) was also opening. Putting a city kid in the middle of this scenario made me quickly think that I had one up on the small city crowd and I would be able to run Vallejo. Soon thereafter, I found out that Vallejo was full of brothas, just like most Bay Area cities of California, and my first impressions were indeed incorrect.

Thinking back, my sixth-grade year was when I met a lot of friends that I still run with today, and these friendships all did not start off too smoothly. Joel and I, for example, fought a bit initially, but it was never anything too serious. We became close friends to the point where his family embraced my mom and me, and we ended up joining our church because of his mother.

Every day after school, we would get into many childish pranks, but never anything serious. With my mom working in Palo Alto, she would leave for work very early in the morning, and during those days, it could be well over a two-hour drive back in the evenings. An idle child with lots of time on his hands in a small city is not the best combination. My friends and I would get into whatever we could, whether it was stealing from stores or discovering more about girls and tongue kissing. Besides the dances that the Boys & Girls Club would have every now and again and football and basketball games, there really wasn't much for kids to do. Sports was a bored mind's refuge, and if you weren't involved in one of them, other extra-curricular activities were bound to get your attention.

Quincey and I ended up on the same baseball team in the 6th grade and are friends to this day. Our friendship extended beyond the field, so much so that when my mom had to stay in a rehab facility, we stayed with Quincey's family. Ironically, when James and my mom broke up, Mom and I found ourselves there once again.

As we got older, my peers and my pranks got bigger. I moved to a neighborhood called College Park when I was fourteen. This was when I became friends with Tremaine (aka Maine) and Chuck. At this time, I was the quarterback on the freshman football team. Maine and Chuck were also on the team. My habits and interests grew, and amongst other things, I started drinking. I remember the day we got drunk off of a 40-ounce of Old English 800 mixed with Thunderbird. After drinking it, I tried to make it home from the park, and I was ripped. My mom, who had by now been sober for a couple years, knew it instantly. She gave me hot water to make me throw up. This wasn't the last time we would test our limit with alcohol. We would get tall cans of St. Ides on the weekends and drink them in the Park late at night. It wasn't about getting drunk for me; it was rising to the challenge and being able to outdrink anyone. I always vowed to not let alcohol be the reason for anything, be it fighting or acting stupid. I always stayed in control of it. It was always Mike, Frank, Hank, sometimes my partner Lil Jackie and I. These are the first people that I started to drink with, and eventually, we would move on to create our deep history of 'firsts.'

The first time I ever bought some dope was from two of my close friends, who were friends from College Park. One, I met in summer school after my 7th-grade year, but we didn't get close until we both moved to College Park. The other actually moved to Vallejo from Frisco. They were my age and doing pretty well in the dope game. So I started learning the game from them. They would come to get me from school at Solano Jr. High School, and we would hit all the tracks in Vallejo and sell as many rocks as possible. In the beginning, I didn't even know how to sell dope. I would spend all my money on food and occasionally on some clothes. As soon as I would sell the dope, I would spend the money, and that was no way to stack cash. Selling crack to kids at school never interested me. In those days, I learned quickly that crack was an adult, blue-collar worker drug or very attractive for a welfare recipient. At the time, school-aged kids were more into weed, but money from weed sales was always too slow unless you were pushing large quantities, whereas, with crack, you could basically quadruple your money in one day. Watching a dope fiend get their welfare check, head to McDonald's and buy their children one meal, and spend the rest of their check with me and my friends kinda had me feeling bad for a minute, but not bad enough to stop. For me, life was good. I was able to buy what I wanted, and at the time, I had a fetish with tennis shoes.

Things kept changing, but one thing remained constant: I was headed for a dead-end street and blinded by my self-created reality that this road was my way to another more lucrative life with more freedom and more choices.

Chapter 3: The Funk Starts

As small and community-oriented as Vallejo was, we were still often divided by turfs and gangs (by police definition, not ours) in the city. So, it comes as no surprise that while growing up there were six or seven major turfs which included: College Park, The Crest, Southside, The Hills, and Hillcrest, to name a few (there are more). For the most part, we all got along until the major funk started between the Crest and The Hills. The problems of the older brothers from the Crest trickled down to the younger generation of the Crest, even though College Park and the Crest were in North Vallejo.

People in my crew got along well with the Crest, but of course, I was always the exception to the rule. Regardless of the peace, I personally had plenty of fights with them, with the major contributors being my big mouth and my fearlessness towards any man. Those nights in training, courtesy of Uncle Corey locking me out on the porch, forced me to be good with my hands. I grew to appreciate that. Lessons well learned.

Our junior high school had developed a reputation for being the roughest in the city. Few school events were drama free, but in spite of that, we looked forward to the dances that we had ever so often. I remember at one of the dances, a local D.J. let some of the kids rap. From our neighborhood (College Park), Dalla D and Mac Ron started to rap. Everybody from College Park was hollering "Parkside" and the people from the Crest didn't like that. Then he let Mac Mall (now a well-known rap artist), who is from the Crest, rap. But with us, it was all good; it didn't bother us at all. After the dance, I made the mistake of not walking home with my boys, and the fellas from the Crest caught me slipping. Someone stole on me and hit me in the face, but while I am stubborn, I am no fool and quickly recognized that there were too many of them, so I kept on walking. When I had gotten to the bottom of the hill, I kind of just had enough, and one of the members who I had a previous altercation with provoked me to want to fight. I didn't need anyone to fan that flame. It was on. After that night, things got pretty intense between us and some folks from the Crest. We had always had separate altercations, but that night was actually the beginning of the drama that would last a few years.

The next few weeks at school went very smooth until one day, the youngsters from the Crest came to school with shirts advertising their new crew called The Ses (short for Sesame Street). This wouldn't have bothered me, but one of the shirts had College Park crossed out on the back, so in my opinion, a line was crossed. It was even more of an issue because that shirt was worn by one of my closest friends at the time. One thing I had really strong love for was College Park. When I saw College Park crossed out, it made me think that the whole purpose of them starting this crew was to get to us, and whether it was or wasn't, that was a problem. I began to crack jokes like where is Big Bird and the Cookie Monster. I had found their hot button. Tension began to rise because of my big mouth.

From that point on, they were out to fight College Park, but they also had a personal vendetta against me. Two days later, one of the people from the Crest started a fight with one of my partners. The next thing you know, I was being jumped. I remember most of the people to this day, and this was in the ninth grade. I only got hit once in the back of the head, and I was laughing the whole time. Many failed attempts were made, but when you talk about College Park, you've opened a can of worms that I will exhaust before I give in. College Park was family to me.

As an athlete, I had two sets of peers. The friends I did dirt with and those I played sports with. Two different mentalities and very different perspectives. The friends I did dirt with were all mostly in high school at this time, and therefore I did not have too much help when I was jumped. You would think this would teach me the lesson that people who say they have my back are not always telling the truth, but it takes a few more times before this sinks in. I learned early on to not blame people for being who they are. There were those who I could fight with and commit crimes with, and there were others who were my social circle. I didn't always completely cut people off for being, either. I simply decided to accept them as they were and expect nothing other than what they had shown me.

My phone was ringing off the hook all night from girls who were checking on me to make sure I was alright and new interested girls who were intrigued by the fact that I was laughing when I got jumped. Funny how amidst the obstacles, life was truly working out in my favor. Popularity on the rise; girls from all walks of life blowing my phone up – and falsely attaching that to masculinity.

Life accelerated over the next few months. I started carrying a gun and knew how to use it if necessary. Funny how learning to shoot a 22-caliber rifle at summer camp would come in handy. Paranoia would set in at times, and I would carry it even at basketball practice. Remaining alert and watching my back every day. I couldn't afford to be caught slipping. After practice, we would head to my house and drink forties and plot how we would get them fools back. Day in and day out, we would have plenty of altercations with the Ses. A lot of times, they would come to the park deep, and we would shoot, or we would have one or two fights and keep moving. I didn't feel overly confident because I had a gun or was part of a turf. My confidence came from knowing that God would protect me and have my back even in the midst of my poor decisions.

I remember a rap group from College Park called B.P. putting out an album, and on the cover of it, they flipped off a sign that had C.C.C. on it. C.C.C. stands for Country Club Crest. Everyone from the Crest was upset by this, and everyone wanted to get revenge.

One Sunday morning, about forty people from the Crest came to College Park, and they wanted to mop (beat down) anyone they saw. They came to the park on bikes, in cars, and on foot. When they got there, my partners Frankie, Sam, Dave C., and Calvin were all there. Nothing major happened because they really couldn't catch anyone. I was not there because I decided to go do some things at the boy's club. Had I been there, who knows what would have happened. I had a big mouth, and I wasn't too big on running. I probably would've been beaten badly. I think about this story and think on how God always spares me from grave danger. This is not the only time God would keep me from harm's way. But still, I remained unchanged.

I can remember days when we would be in the apartment grinding (that's what we call selling dope), and fools from the Crest would come through and shoot dice with us and even buy dope from some of us. Then a week or so later, we would be fighting and feuding again. It was normal back then that during calm periods, enemies and friends alike would shoot dice together and sell each other dope. At the end of the day, we were all from North Vallejo, and we all liked money.

Growing up in the V-town juvenile hall was an experience most of us had in common. At some point in time, we were there. My first stay in juvenile hall was as a result of an altercation between the Crest and College Park. We had a minimum day at school where we got out an hour or two early, and many of us would go eat at a fast food restaurant. Earlier that day, I had an encounter with one of the brothers from the Ses, and they remembered it in the afternoon. When I got to Taco Bell, I heard one of them say, "Shamann came all the way to Taco Bell to get beat up," after which I was jumped again. This time they got me pretty good, and I still didn't have the sense to run.

The first thing I did was go back to our high school and get my partner Mike to take me to the park. At this time, we had a clubhouse that we built behind a dead-end street in College Park, where we had bunk beds and kept about three guns in there. I had Mike take me back to get the .38 revolver, as I was determined to get revenge, and I definitely wasn't going to be jumped again.

Later that night, I called a couple of girls I was friends with to see if they would keep the gun in their locker for me at school the next day. I was as quick on my feet as I was in strategizing a Plan A and B. They both said they would do it, so I knew the gun was coming with me to school the next morning.

When I got dressed that morning, I threw on my College Park hat, grabbed the strap, and headed out. On the way, we stopped at the liquor store to play video games. While at the store, a couple of people from the Ses (including some from the previous day) came to the store. While walking into the store, one of them said, "I'll take your hat." When he came out the store, they didn't say anything to me. I asked him when was he going to take it. Yes, I was usually the one provoking a situation to keep a man at his word. They all proceeded to surround me. I then pulled out my strap, and they backed up. One of them kept hollering, "shoot me." I realized at that moment that I had full control of the situation. I had the power. After about a minute or so and with a small crowd watching, they ran off, and I proceeded to walk to school. My partner Little Jackie, who was with me, kept telling me I was a savage for what I had done.

The man at the store had to have called the police and given a description because shortly thereafter, a policeman stopped us and began to search me immediately. Initially, I wasn't nervous as I thought I had a solid case. A gun case never even crossed my mind here. I really just thought I would be able to go back to school, as I had no clue about the seriousness of a gun charge until later; this was merely an act of self-defense. Plus, I didn't have any real fear in my young mind. After the officer found the gun, I was arrested, and he took me to the police station, and in my naivety, I thought I would still be going back to school later on that day. From there, I was taken to juvenile hall and had no idea what to expect. I didn't know how long I would be there or what would happen once I got there. I just knew I was prepared to fight somebody if they tried to rape me or pick on me.

I quickly realized that the hall was nothing like the thoughts I had quickly conjured. I practically knew everybody in there, and besides that, we didn't get a chance to spend that much time outside of our rooms. In the Solano County Juvenile Hall, we didn't get much freedom to roam about. People just talked about what they had done and when they were going home or when they were going to be transferred. Ironically, being locked up was actually working out to my advantage. Going to the hall was like being awarded stripes or awards in the hood for my wrongdoing. This told people that I had been locked up and wasn't afraid to do anything. This is how it works in the streets.

Being around people who I knew made this place slightly familiar, but still, the mystery of the unknown kept me awake a bit longer than usual that night. I was in my own room. No cells in juvenile hall as they don't want to make it seem like the penitentiary in order to keep it youth friendly, for lack of a better term. Juvenile hall is not supposed to feel like a prison, at least not back in those days), so I didn't have to watch my back, but I did think about everything I was missing out on. Freedom being at the top of my list.

In court the next morning, I was initially detained; however, released to my mother by an intake officer within a few hours. My mother was not the kind of parent to give me the silent treatment; on the contrary, she wanted to talk everything out. This offense, of course, was no different, and she wanted to talk even more about the direction my life was beginning to take and the consequences of my actions. Buried in my own thoughts, I had almost completely tuned her completely out, but just paying enough attention to catch the odd word or two. Consequences? What consequences? I was being identified as the guy from College Park who pulled the gun out on the way to school. I spent the night in juvenile hall, and now I was a free man. Life was good. There was no price to pay; my reputation on the streets had just received a 'stamp of approval.' Well, that's what I thought then.

Chapter 4: The System

During the next few years of my life, trouble with the law continued. On one of the occasions when I had just been released from juvenile hall, my partners and I went to a party at this girl's house. There were a lot of people there from College Park and the Crest. We outnumbered the Crest that night, but some of the people with us ran, and my friend got jumped. By the time I got over there, the police came and broke up the chaos. I was irked by their decision to leave one of our friends when he needed us. That is something I simply could not do, nor did it sit well with me, but it helped to bring home the point that people show you time and time again where you are in their life when I may have placed them elsewhere. No one is perfect, and therefore everyone will let you down at some point. My defense mechanism had desensitized me; I had now expected people to fail me.

After the police came and broke up the fight, we went outside and saw two Caprice Classics that we liked. We broke a piece in the steering column and used a screwdriver to pull the ignition. It was on. We drove off with two Classics and rolled through the Crest. Once again, God was on my side because we got shot at on Taper Street, but the bullets missed. The car was riddled with bullet holes, but we weren't fazed. At the time, I used to think it was cute to be shot at; after all, I continuously lived to talk about it. I somehow felt like I was winning. We were so comfortable with our ability to stay ahead of the game that my partner Mac and I became distracted with something as trivial as who was going to drive the car (a stolen car at that). While we were arguing, the police pulled up, unknown to us, and caught some of the people in the other car. Once again, I escaped danger and another chance at incarceration. A guardian angel was watching over me. Two of my friends got away that night, but the next day somebody broke the code and gave up the info. Snitching is an unforgivable act in the streets.

That summer became even more hectic for me. Initially, I wasn't really heavy into the dope game, but as time progressed, I became more involved in a major way, and with the money I was making, I was hooked. This was around the same time my mom moved us from College Park, closer to downtown Vallejo. I hated the move, but my rebellious tendencies didn't fight her on this. That decision more than likely may have been one of my biggest blessings in disguise, which has also made me wonder at times about a mother's sixth sense. Did she see bigger trouble coming? Have a hunch to make it more difficult for me to find trouble? Some call it a coincidence. I call it God. Whatever it was that made her move us right at that very moment contributed to me deciding not to go to the park one day. That same day, I received a call that four of my closest friends had pulled a drive-by on some people from the Ses. No one was killed, but one of the members of the Ses was shot. Had I been there, I would have more than likely shot someone and possibly killed someone. God spared me from that, and I am forever grateful to Him. Three of my friends went to the California Youth Authority (C.Y.A.)—which is a prison for juveniles—for the shooting, and my other friend did some time in juvenile hall.

To this day, I can't help but think it was my fault they went to jail. I was partly to blame for the entire mess. From what I heard, they came to the park fifteen deep, and I was one of the people they came looking for that day. What sparked the shooting was a fight that my friend got into with one of my former friends, who I was really close to in the SES. One of them stole on (sucker punched) one of my close friends, and because my friends were outnumbered, they let the Ses leave and came back firing (shooting). I have never shared this with anyone, but deep down, I have always blamed myself for what happened that day. God had kept me away from there and away from

C.Y.A. (and possibly a life of incarceration), but to come to terms with the fact that I was part of the reason that three of my partners went to jail bothered me.

All my friends went to jail, which made me begin to stay close to the house as it wasn't the right time to be hanging out by myself. My partner Greg and I kicked it tight that summer. One thing about the Ses, they always popped up when you least expected it. One night they caught me slipping by myself at a party. They kept heckling me by saying that they were going to get me good and kept it going with reminders that everyone who had my back was locked up. This is the only night I have retreated in my entire life, and decided to leave with one of Greg's friends, who had their mom pick us up. With the Ses, you just never knew, and they now outnumbered us by at least seven to one. I decided to go get another gun just to be on the safe side but changed my mind when the summer continued without any trouble.

Tenth-grade year marked the beginning of greater troubles. With the exception of a couple weeks on the junior varsity baseball team, I didn't play any sports. Chuck and I got really close, and before you knew it, we were always together. His family fully accepted me and his mother became my second mother. Every day it was Chuck and I selling dope. We used to get quarter ounces for about $150.00. Anyone who has ever sold dope knows that is a great price, and with business thriving, we decided to buy quarter ounces instead of moving up to half ounces and ounces. On really good days, we would get two or three. Every day we hit school and then the track all night. Every weekend we would hit the mall and get fitted. We thought we had it made. I used some of the money to help my mom. TVs, cable boxes, and many other items from dope fiends contributed to the household, and there were times when I would chip in and buy the groceries. It felt good to be able to help, and the biggest thing for me was that my mom didn't have to buy me things. I couldn't get anything too lavish for her, though. She was pretty witty, and I didn't want to unnecessarily raise any eyebrows. So there were times that I had money, but I had to play it off like I didn't have any just to keep her at bay.

When the summertime hit, it was really on. I had a learner's permit, and about two weeks into summer, I bought a 1969 Chevrolet Bel-Air. People speculated how I was able to afford a car. Some asked, but most people just read between the lines. Hell, when I first got my car, my mom didn't even have one at the time. After this, there was no stopping me.

We did things that would continue to defy logic. One night my partner Mike showed me how to steel Ford Mustangs and Cougars with just a wire and a hanger. After finding this out, we had a plan to go around stealing Mustangs and Cougars, and then we were going to sell them. Now looking back, I don't really know why we were trying to steal cars when I already had one. We went out to Pinole and tried to take our first one and got caught up. My partners Greg, Chuck, and I got arrested. Mike got away because he was in my car. This time we went to a juvenile hall in Contra Costa County. This is the county where Richmond and Martinez people go to jail, and by nature, Vallejo and Richmond brothers don't get along. When I first got there, I thought I was going to be in there fighting all day, but the first couple of days were cool. After about four days, I got transferred to the girls' unit because of overcrowding, and I felt that was pretty cool. I thought then that life was truly making the best of a bad situation. The counselors kept a close eye on me, and I wasn't allowed to be alone with the girls. One day later, Greg got transferred to the unit where I was, and Chuck got to go home because it was his first offense.

I went to court a couple of times, but I never admitted to doing anything. Greg and I had the same probation officer, and she was not letting us get released. I couldn't wait to get out. One day in court, the judge released Greg and sent me back to the hall. However, later that day, I was released. My mother came to pick me up with one of the reverends from church. I swore up and down, down and up, that I was not going back to the hall.

Months prior to this incarceration, people kept telling me how beautiful my daughter was. I began to grow even more curious as to the real truth. If there is anyone I know who can get the true story out of someone, it is my mother. So when I told mom that I think I may have a daughter, without hesitation, she picked up the phone and asked for the truth, which then came freely. I went over to my daughter's mother's house and saw and held her for the first time a few days after she was born. Understandably the father of my mother's daughter was on my case but respected the fact that I came to their home to see my child and introduce myself. Holding my daughter during those first few minutes filled me with the responsibility of needing to do right by my daughter, but in my young mind, I didn't really have a full understanding of what that meant. After that, I went to the track and got back on the grind. I guess I still didn't learn my lesson.

For the rest of that summer, I continued to prosper in my mind. I stayed drunk and kept hanging with people who I thought were my friends. This summer seemed different, though; I would spend time with my daughter on weekends and some evenings. My mother and her maternal grandparents were extremely supportive of our efforts and never created a hostile environment or tried to keep her away from me, which has always been a blessing. At the end of the summer, it was time for football season.

I think that football practice and my daughter kept me out of trouble for a little while. When school started back, I was ready. I had a car, money, and hella new clothes. Every day, we had football practice, and as much as I loved the game, I felt that it was cramping my style, and sitting on the bench, in my case, was not something I was used to. After three games of football, I was kicked off of the team for causing trouble on the way back from an away game in Napa. The very next night, I was out doing dirt again. A couple of my partners, Lil Jack, Mike, Mack, Chuck, myself, and someone else I can't recall, were out in Benicia, CA, looking for someone to rob. This always seemed so easy, so when we found an easy target, two of my friends got out the car and robbed him.

We pulled off and forgot to turn on the lights, and the police pulled us over. When he stopped us, he heard on the radio that someone had just been robbed. They made us all get out the car and lined us up right there. The man who was robbed said that I was the one who got out the car and pulled out the gun on him. That was not true, but nevertheless, I was charged with armed robbery and possession of a firearm. At the police station, I told them that I had never even gotten out of the car, but that didn't matter to them. They took me to juvenile hall once again.

This time I was once again headed to the hall in Solano County, but this time I wasn't alone because they sent Chuck and me together. Seemed like our lives ran parallel: people thought we looked alike, we had daughters that were born within months of each other, we did dirt together, and always had each other's back. I really wasn't worried about anything since I had my road dog with me. I assumed I would go to court about twice a week, but this time my probation officer decided against releasing me. Maybe it was the feeling on their part that I had become so immune to my frequent troubles with the law and consequences that paled in comparison that this time it shouldn't be as predictable. Even though I pleaded innocent, the fact that I was identified in a line-up basically negated anything I had to say and sealed the thought with the judge that I was guilty before trial. The district attorney tried to get me to plead guilty, but that would've probably gotten me sent to C.Y.A. (California Youth Authority), which is a penitentiary for juveniles. This was definitely somewhere I didn't want to be, especially for something that I didn't do.

Another issue was the fact that I had to switch public defenders during my case, which meant I had to get more time in between court dates. If I was willing to tell the police who really committed the robbery, I would have been set free, but I just wasn't raised like that; in the hood, we didn't snitch; plus, I shouldn't have been there. I would rather go to trial for a crime I didn't commit than be labeled a snitch.

After six weeks in the Intense Security Unit in juvenile hall, I finally went to trial. When I got to court, I was happy to see that my partner Lil Jackie who sat next to me in the car, was there to testify for me. The main problem with my case was the fact that nobody was going to say who really committed the crime. Lil Jack was just going to say he was asleep and that I couldn't have got out the car without him waking up because he was lying on my shoulder. Chuck couldn't be there to testify because his case was pending. So nobody else could testify. A couple of my partners came through as character witnesses.

When my trial started, I couldn't understand what my lawyer and the D.A. were talking about, which only led to more frustration. I was ready to go home but not desperate enough to spill the beans. Six weeks to some people is nothing, but I was ready to be free. The hall was so boring, and you spent most of the time locked in your room. When my lawyer and the D.A. finished talking, the bailiff came over and started taking off my handcuffs. I was released to my mother and Pelton Stewart (the Executive Director of the Omega Boys and Girls Club at the time).

It turns out that the person who was robbed didn't show up for court. My lawyer (actually public defender) and the D.A. were arguing because the D.A. wanted to keep me in custody and change the trial date. The judge said that the D.A. had no case without a witness, so I was released. All of this took place over twelve dollars and a watch. Most of us could've made that in half of a crack sale, but more importantly, it would not have been worth it if I got sent to the C.Y.A.

Once again, God was on my side, but my lesson still wasn't learned. I got out on December 3rd, 1991, and managed to stay cool for a couple of months. By March 1992, I was back to selling dope once again. I tried my best to stay out of trouble, but I wanted things that my mom couldn't afford to buy me. I couldn't deal with seeing everyone else with fresh tennis shoes and not having them myself.

This time I was doing pretty good on the dope track. I knew how to stack my money, but I developed another problem: shooting dice. At first, I would just shoot for ($1's) dollars. Pretty soon, I went to $5s, $10s, and $20s, and I have even shot for $100s at some point. Like a lot of my habits, gambling quickly became an addiction for me. After a while, I started losing a lot of money, and my partners, Lil Jackie and Dae-Dae, would tell me that I would go broke if I didn't stop. The idea of going from five dollars to two hundred dollars in ten minutes was just too appealing for me to stop. On the one hand, I was the person supplying crack to addicts, saw them go to any length to get their hands on it, and now the roles had reversed. I was the addict, and my drug of choice was gambling. At times I did go broke. Every time I was down to nothing, my partners would give me a loan, and I would get back on my feet.

I really thought I had it good now, money in my pocket and plenty of clothes. One day I was grinding, and I had served this lady a twenty piece (twenty dollars of rock cocaine). When she left, I hesitated to put my rocks back in the bushes because a car was coming. I didn't trust anybody, so I wanted to wait for the car to pass before I hid my dope again. As the car got closer, I noticed a police officer that I had dealt with before. Without even thinking, I took off through the park, and both of the policemen in the car chased me. When I hit a corner in the park, I threw my dope in the bushes and ran to where everyone was playing basketball, and I sat down. I wanted to be in a crowded area because I knew when you make the police chase you, they get mad and are more prone to beating you pretty badly when they catch you. In the midst of a crowded area, that was less likely to happen. I was always strategizing.

While I was sitting there, one of the officers grabbed me and handcuffed me. He then went to search for the dope but couldn't find it. I just knew I was off the hook, and they sensed that might be the case which further infuriated them. All of a sudden, the other officer went back to look one more time, and when he returned, he had the dope with him.

On the way to the police station, I was questioned about the dope. I just kept telling them that the dope wasn't mine. They said I needed to cooperate or the consequences would be greater. I still didn't budge. When I got to the police station, they lost their minds and asked me who did I get my dope from. They should have known better than to think I would have given up that information. The whole time I just knew I was washed and on my way to the boys' ranch or C.Y.A. To my surprise, they wrote me a citation and sent me home. Had I been sent to juvenile hall, I do not know where I would be today. Once again, God had his angels around me, and it was almost as if I kept pushing Him in disbelief that He would always be there for me. Either that, or I was so foolish to believe that I was invincible and would always escape the wrath of stupidity. When I got home, I was mad that they took my dope and went right back to the track to get some more. I bought a hundred pop with some money I had at the house. Was it that I was fearless or senseless? I just caught a dope case and went right back to the track. One thing I didn't lack then was perseverance. If only I could reverse my focus and use it more on the good that needed to get done.

Chapter 5: A Mother's Love

By the time the summer of 1992 hit, things had escalated. From not going home at night to sometimes spending the night out grinding and selling_dope and grabbing a quick shut-eye in a friend's car, I was out of control. It was as if I had become immune to the danger of the streets, be it fools from out of town robbing me or a dope fiend high on the very drug I sold them taking my life. It would have been written that I lost my life over foolishness or really greed from my own addiction to money. More and more money. Sleeping in the car allowed me to run a 24hr operation, vying to not miss any sales regardless of the time of day or night. No gun and with little sleep, the only thing I could see was the endless opportunities. The risks were many, but I saw the rewards as being more.

I still had my dope case pending auto theft cases and was going to court regularly. One day, my friend Toni was giving me a ride to my court appearance, and I had a strange feeling I just couldn't shake. Before getting out of her car, I gave her my dope and told her to give it to my partner in case something happened. Looking back, this was probably from the voice of reason asking me what the hell was I doing with dope on me about to go to court anyway. It was July 1st, 1992, which meant that it would be a great day for business. The first of the month is usually a big day for all dope dealers because that's when a lot of people who used drugs got paid. I had my day all mapped out as to where and how my time would be spent after my meeting with the judge.

When I walked into the courtroom, I first saw my mom and my probation officer, which I found quite odd. My mom had told me the night prior that she wasn't coming to court for me due to an argument we had, so when I saw her, I just felt she had a change of heart. What I couldn't understand at the time was why my probation officer, who was never usually here, chose to show up today. Something strange was going on.

When the court got in session, the judge called the case to order, and my probation officer and the judge had a conversation. Before I knew it, I was on my way back to the Hall because my probation officer told the judge I wasn't coming home at night and that they should detain me, and they did. The strange feeling I was having all day, began to make sense. I was enraged. The bailiff arrested me and then searched me but found nothing. Once again, God was trying to give me another chance to get myself together. If I had not given my dope to Toni, my problems at this point would have been even worse.

What I didn't know was that my mom was telling my probation officer that I wasn't coming home at night all along and that she found drugs and money in my room. Though it was all true, how could a mother do that to her own son? She violated the mother-child code. This I could not understand.

On my way to the hall, my mind was full of anger and hate for my mother. I could not understand how she could snitch on her own child and do it on the 1st of the month, which was a huge money day for any dope dealer. I vowed to never again love or talk to her.

The problem with my hatred at the time was that there was no way I could get out of juvenile hall without my mother wanting me back home. So as always, I needed her, and regardless of my pent-up anger towards her, I had to act like we were on good terms.

This time at the hall, I was locked up with a lot of people who were from the Ses. By now, we were way past our petty discrepancies, and things between us all were pretty much cool. I didn't trust them, but we got along. All the counselors knew who I was, which was a clear indication that I had been here too many times, so it was more of a welcome home that gave me access to certain privileges that I wasn't supposed to have. I could get out of my room when I wanted to, and I was able to stay up later than everyone else. I only spent six days in there this time, but I missed out on making a lot of money on the 1st of the month.

I was released on home supervision which meant that I had to be in the house by eight o'clock on the weekdays and by nine o'clock on the weekends. Talk about cramping my business – but with me, obstacles were just a way for me to strategize a new game plan. I learned how to exercise my brain power early on.

In the daytime, I would sell some dope, and then I would go to this girl's house who I was dating who had her own place. Besides hanging out with her, this became a meeting spot for my friends and me where we could eat and drink before going home. The county was supposed to call me every night to make sure that I was home at the correct time. I no longer trusted my mother to be on my side, so I made sure I was home when I was supposed to be every day. My last court visit had struck a chord with me, but I still had yet to learn my lesson.

Unknown to my friends and me at the time, while I was in juvenile hall, undercover policemen rode through the park and bought dope. Everybody who sold dope to them was on camera. We started putting the pieces together through the series of events that followed. One night, while we went to the Solano County Fair one of my friends was arrested right at the fair. Two days earlier, another one of my friends was arrested. Both of them had been on camera. I remember how mad I was on July 1st when I sat in court, and my mother had shattered the parent-child confidentiality agreement I thought all parents emotionally signed. Not that I was then prepared to tell her thank you for sparing me from greater troubles, but I did acknowledge that once again, the Lord wanted me to be kept out of harm's way, and since I did not have the discipline or good judgment to make wise choices when allowed freedom, He took that choice away temporarily to ensure I was where I was supposed to be. Had I not been sitting in juvenile hall during this time, I would have caught another dope case and for sure would have been sent to C.Y.A.

Many arrests took place at the end of July, and when we thought the wave of arrests had come to an end that summer, my friend Tremaine was arrested in September because he had been caught on camera also. They couldn't find him earlier because he had no prior criminal record. Of all my friends, I really didn't want Tremaine to sell dope in the first place, but he's so stubborn that he did it anyway.

After those sweeps took place, another chord was struck, and I started to seriously think about my life and where I was headed. I wanted to at least start heading in another direction, but I just wasn't sure how willing I was to take the first turning steps toward change. Only time would tell if I was willing to pay the price of living the *straight and narrow* to get there.

As angry as I was with my mother for making one of the most difficult decisions any parent has to make, I was that much more thankful that she listened to the direction from God to have me locked up. My mother saw me heading for danger and acted. I thank God for her decision to this day.

My mother always did the best she could for me. We didn't have much, but we always got by. She has been through so much unnecessarily because of me. Missing days from work to come to my court hearings, receiving calls from schools and having her co-workers know I was in trouble once again, having her credit ruined to try to keep me in brand-name clothes. Back in those days, none of this stuff registered in my thought process.

My mom has been through so much. I have watched her be abused by my father and some of her boyfriends. I have watched her spend the only money she had to make sure that I had something to eat, and she was so strong through it all. Catherine Cartwright (my mother) had no help with raising me for so many years. Trying to raise a young man by herself was not an easy task, especially one who did nothing to make it easier for her.

My mother never attests to being an angel, but she has always done what she could for me. She feels guilty to this day for moving me around a lot, but she wanted to keep me out of San Francisco. That's why she moved me to Mountain View, Vallejo, and Fremont when I was much younger. I still managed to get in all of the trouble I could have in a small city like Vallejo.

Growing up, it was just my mother and me most of the time. Watching a woman break her back to raise you is something I don't wish on any child. Yet and still, as a teenager, I managed to stress her out with my issues, with no apathy for her own.

Chapter 6: Philmore Graham And Atlanta, GA

My mischievous countenance to the side, academics remained on my radar. I was always intrigued by expanding my capacity and, of course, in everything, saw it as a competition of sorts. In between trouble and freedom, I was a member of the Continentals of Omega Boys and Girls Club, an organization that differed from many others due to its strong focus on academics.

This boys and girls club was founded by a man by the name of Philmore Graham – (PG), who is also a member of the Omega Psi Phi Fraternity Inc. His vision was to have a place for young black males to go and receive training based on four principles: brotherhood (later to include sisterhood as well), scholarship, perseverance, and uplift. He also wanted these young men to have a place where they could do their homework and expand their horizons by going on trips together and seeing a world beyond the familiar. Equally important, he wanted this place to have a sense of home, operating as a family unit under one roof. Over the years, all this and much more have been accomplished. Now the boys and girls club has a roster of thousands of members, and hundreds of them are in colleges and universities all over the country, not to mention the hundreds who have already obtained college degrees.

Philmore Graham was more than just the founder of the boys and girls club; he played the active role of mentor, life coach, role model and served as the permanent male presence in the lives of children under his care who missed that voice on the home front. On numerous occasions, he has put the children of the boys and girls club ahead of his own well-being. I can speak to this personally as he would, at times, pick me up after school or on weekends, always trying to keep me very preoccupied with odd jobs that inevitably kept me away from the temptation of selling dope. When I did manage to find myself in trouble with the law, PG was the person my mom would call, and regardless of the hour, he was ever present to accompany her on the exhausting journey to pick me up. Not once or twice, but countless times.

His role in my life cannot be summed up in words on paper, but who I have become and a great deal of the things I learned along the way is a testament to the greatness of a man who is not biologically my father but who raised me as if he was. This is a role he played in the lives of many kids, in addition to being very active in the lives of his own children and life partner to his spouse. To know him is to recognize his unique ability to meet people from all walks of life, develop those relationships beyond the surface, and serve in the role of mentor without the formality. He wanted you to succeed greater than you could at that specific time, and with his forward-thinking kept you focused on what you could do versus all that you had done. The soul of a good man is easily defined as one who takes another's child as his own. In my eyes, PG is the epitome of a great man who took many children under his care simply because he saw a little spark that he felt, if given an opportunity, could increase beyond its sheltered space in the world.

It's quite funny how we met. One day while I was at my worst behavior with the staff at the Boys and Girls Club, PG saw the entire situation unfold. It would only make sense that someone whose presence would very quickly have a profound effect on my life would meet me when I was on the verge of being at my worst. There must have been something that PG saw in me after that conversation, as he automatically took a more vested interest in bringing out the best I had to offer, pulling from the very qualities I misused to travel down the road well-traveled in the hood. Somewhere in between life as usual and the road to a better place, PG tested me as he does with most people. Really a tactic he uses to gauge your level of intelligence.

34

After asking me a few questions when we first met and listening to my responses, he noticed that the foundation was there; it was simply a matter of reversing how my skill set was being used. Though he pushed education, he was far from one-dimensional. He knew how to have fun and knew how to keep the attention of the youth. To his credit, his versatility made him comfortable in any setting. Whether he was in the hood, in congress, dealing with the kids at the club, or trying to find me in the streets, this educated black man had a presence about him that made him able to work with people from any walk of life.

Aside from moral support, PG has also been there for me financially. He would never just give me money, but he would let me earn it by working in the backyard. Sometimes he would give me money for my grades. Even when I tried to shake PG, he wouldn't give up on me. While I was out there in the streets, he would come after me to keep me in line. I can remember days when I was on track, and PG would come get me. I also remember stealing a car and getting arrested, and my mom calling PG in the middle of the night. He came to get me from the police station, and I lied to him the whole night. After a while, he got the truth out of me. No one else has been able to have that effect on me. Somehow he always knew what I was doing, but I would still try to lie about everything. In spite of all my efforts to keep him at bay and putting him through all types of rings and hoops, he still stuck by me. His concern for me was unconditional. No one in the community, not my mother, not the other boys and girls club members, fully grasped the extent of the relationship between PG and me. Though I grew up without the presence of my real father, God gave me one in a man who caught a glimpse of me at my worst and was up to the challenge of turning my life around and welcomed me into his family. Sometimes the water is thicker than blood.

After the sweep that July, where all my friends went to jail, I had a chance to experience something that changed my life forever. The

Omega Psi Phi Fraternity, Inc. was holding a youth leadership conference at their bi-annual conclave in Atlanta, GA. Only five club members were going to be chosen to go, and these would be selected based on who the committee felt would represent the club well and additionally were among the more active members in the Keystone group – which is the club's leadership group. Even though I stayed in trouble, I still went to Keystone meetings on a Thursday just so I could be around Mr. Graham and get all the information he had to offer. Now truth be told, the odds were against me being chosen to go, and not because of some distant trouble I had gotten myself into from years gone by, but I was just getting out of juvenile hall a couple weeks prior to everyone leaving. Sometimes our life or the lives of our loved ones run parallel to someone we meet in life. That connection gives us a different perspective which tends to delve beyond the surface when deciding what a possible change agent could be. Mr. Graham's son Montoya had gotten into a lot of trouble when he was growing up as well, but at his turning point, he took the road to Tennessee State University because he was given a glimpse of life outside of our world as we knew it. Montoya believed that if I went on that trip, there was a possibility I would change; he also believed that if I didn't go, my life was headed toward a dead end. That, coupled with whatever it was that PG saw in me, echoed louder than the voices around him saying no, and I was on that flight headed to Atlanta, GA, with my friend Mario, Bobby Brooks, Eddie Jackson, and Tyrone.

When I got to the conference, it was a completely different world for me. I saw a world I didn't even know existed. There were lots of intelligent black men functioning in a capacity that did not include guns or drugs, and it was evident that they cared about their communities. They were well put together with top-of-the-line cars, impeccably dressed, and with mates by their side of equal measure. They seemed to have acquired this legally, which was not the norm for me. They piqued my interest, and I wanted to find out what got

36

them to these esteemed positions. They indulged me with dialogue and shared that the secret was really an education. All I have to do is go to college? Really? Really. All the workshops we attended, the Omega men we came in contact with, and the professors and students we met while visiting HBCU campuses stressed the value of an education. But it didn't seem like it was abnormal. On the contrary, it seemed that they knew this all along and success, professionally and personally, was their level of expectation. The irony was that I had been around financially successful people almost my entire life, but these were dope dealers, hustlers, bank robbers, and all sorts of lucrative "careers" which enabled them to acquire wealth in a different way. What I was around had framed my ideas on how to become successful, and here were people showing me another way through applying my academic strengths and getting a college degree. My horizons had been broadened. My life changed.

What also struck a chord with me was that there were such a large number of black men in one setting, and there were no altercations. It seemed that every time we got together in California, an issue was guaranteed. This wasn't the case in Atlanta. In the midst of thousands, there was a sense of camaraderie, and everyone was getting along.

I would not be me without pointing out the last noticeable difference from my trip. There was a plethora of beautiful and educated black women in Atlanta. Being in Vallejo and the Bay Area, you often see beautiful women representing all races and ethnicities, but not that magnitude of beautiful black women.

Seeing all of this made me realize that there was another side to what I had known as life up to this point. We talked about these possibilities at the boys and girls club, but to actually bear witness to the reality that it did indeed exist was life-changing. . Many of us in Vallejo thought that everything we heard just wasn't a reality for us.

Seeing this made me determined to change this not only for myself but for others in my circle and community.

On my way back to Vallejo, I decided that I was going to attend a historically black college and that what I had just experienced would also become my reality someday.

As I type this chapter, Philmore Graham, or PG as he is called by many, is suffering from dementia, and it saddens me to think that our unsung hero may not consciously see the fruits of his labor from all the lives he has changed and actually saved throughout the years. The seeds of transformation have been planted. May the farmer know the fruits only made it to due season because he tilled the soil even during the times of drought.

Chapter 7: The Transformation

I got back from my trip and exhausted all my conversations with stories of what I had experienced in Atlanta. My friends got tired of hearing about my trip, but I wanted to replay the images I had seen and sell them on the idea of moving south to Atlanta. I was now better able to understand the excitement that Uncle Corey had when he was leaving for Morris Brown College. I remember that day like it was yesterday. Mom, my partner Quincey and I met up with Corey's friends at the airport to see him off as he headed south to school. Back in those days, you were able to go to the actual gate with the passengers, and that day, as we watched this young black man take the continued steps towards greater educational aspirations, the energy at the gate was simply electric. I heard his stories coupled with tales from others who had made it to colleges and universities around the country, but it wasn't until I had a front-row seat and saw it all with my own eyes that it came full circle. The stories they had told us at the Boys & Girls Club turned out to be factual, and this life was actually someone's reality. Now I saw that I could be that someone. While on the streets, my reality was framed by the hustle that this is all there is and the only way to having more. In one trip with a different landscape, I saw that there was more, and with education came exposure on so many other levels.

My reality at the time was that I still had many things to face at home. I had to get off of probation and stop selling dope. Equally challenging for me would be denying the call to get back in the game when I got the nudge to return to a life I knew oh so well. It's ironic that drug dealers watch their customers day in and day out give in to temptation and feed their inner craving for a drug they think they cannot live without, while on the other hand, the dealer who tries to walk away battles his own demons. The most powerful of which is not to give in to his own temptations. This time though, I was determined to walk away. Walk the straight and narrow as much as I could because what I had seen had proven that there was more to life than where I was and what I was doing. The drastic redirection it would now take to get on a different track was worth the sacrifice. The question I had to be mindful of was could I make all these changes and still hang with the same crowd? With not too much time on my hands to turn over a few new leaves, I realized I only had my senior year of high school to make it all happen. The blessing in disguise was that all along, I had kept decent grades.

The first thing I did was stop grinding (selling dope), which was very hard for me. I still needed money, and for some reason, I had issues with working a traditional job which I tied to my lack of patience, which was really an excuse to be lazy. I did everything I could to stay away from the grind.

Changing my friends or really lessening the time spent in any circles that may have led me back down a road I was no longer trying to travel along was also easy to do. I had always had two sets of friends. Ones I did dirt with and ones I played sports with. That year, I stuck tight with the friends I played sports with but don't be mistaken when you're trying to make a drastic change in your life; temptation drifts even closer and remains ever present. Mixed in with the athletes were guys who had also sold dope and had been locked up. At the time, it just seemed that selling dope and going to juvenile hall was the thing to do in Vallejo. Every day we would just go to school and then kick it on the weekends. Since I didn't play any sports my senior year (except for baseball for a Senior Babe Ruth League), I also spent most of my days in the company of girls, which played a major role in helping to keep me out of legal trouble.

The hardest thing to do was to get out of the system and off probation. Even with all of my changes, I was still no angel. Once you're in the system, it is hard as hell to get out. As many changes as

I had made, this wasn't to be confused with me being willing to sit back and be shoved around. That being said, one day during my senior year, I was watching a fight after school one day. Police came, and they started trying to get everyone to back up, myself included. I refused, and so one of them pushed me back. I immediately took offense to that and began to curse him out for touching me. I was then wrestled into a police car and taken to the police station. After a couple of hours there, I was released to the custody of my mother. Once again, I had to see the shame in my already stressed-out mother's face.

I tried to sue the policeman for police brutality, but of course, I didn't have a case. That incident alone got me three more months' probation. Getting out of the system had definitely become my biggest struggle.

The right inspiration will keep the biggest struggles at bay, I have learned. So besides going to the boys and girls club on Thursday nights, I now attended the youth group at church on Wednesday nights. I want to also thank Edison Kelly—now Dr. Kelly—for always picking me up on those Wednesday nights. I was doing everything I could in an effort to stay out of trouble. I even got my first real girlfriend in my senior year of high school. Safe to say that my days of trouble with the law were becoming a shadow of my past, and I was turning the corner to a new chapter in my life.

I knew I had a few odds against me, so to make sure I had the best foot forward; I dedicated quality time to filling out college applications. The energy I once invested in selling dope was now being redirected to get me into school. PG was there every step of the way. He truly invested a sincere interest in doing everything he could to make sure children – whether his or not – had a chance of a better life or, at the very least, were exposed to life-changing opportunities. He instituted a policy at the boys and girls club that the club would cover the application fees for any of its members who applied to colleges and universities. No limitations and no investigation into the students' past or their socio-economic background. He was just that kind of person. At times the club did not actually have the funds for the applications that were being submitted, and rather than PG crushing a child's dream, he dipped into his own pockets to give another man's child the chance of a successful life. The lives he helped change and the dreams he helped bring to fruition are too many to note. With someone, a stranger really, who is that committed to your success, how could you fail? How would you ever be able to look them boldly in the eyes without feeling some kind of guilt for not being as committed to extracting your own potential?

I took the S.A.T. twice and made sure I applied to several schools to keep my options open. The relief for me was that the club was paying for it, as I could not imagine asking my mom to pay all those application fees all at once. Of course, my former lifestyle, though lucrative, was not an option. Too close and too much of a risk to take. All these schools were Historically Black Colleges and Universities, and the list included Alabama State University, Morris Brown College, Tennessee State University, Tuskegee University, Langston University, and Clark Atlanta University. I wrestled with whether or not my first choice should be Morris Brown College or Tuskegee based solely on the debt issues facing Morris Brown at the time. Tuskegee then became my number-one choice.

I intentionally spent a lot more time with PG during my senior year. I really did everything I could to keep myself around positivity and still, to this day, intentionally surround myself with positive influences. I won't sit here and tell you I was a perfect angel my senior year because I still kept drinking Mad Dog 20/20, 40 ounces of malt liquor, and Carlos Rossi every weekend. As soon as it was Friday, I was at the liquor store.

Every time I thought about doing something stupid, I would get some type of sign from God to stay on the straight and narrow. I can remember wanting to grind and then coming home and receiving my first acceptance letter to college. This one came from Morris Brown. Then I received acceptance letters from Alabama State, Langston University, and Tuskegee. As good as those acceptance letters felt, those two rejection letters from Clark Atlanta University and Tennessee State University hurt. To let you in on a little secret, Tennessee State University was really my first choice. That was where PG, his son Montoya and his daughter Diedre went to school. With my track record, I was still happy to be on the receiving end of acceptance letters. With each one, my dream was being kept alive.

Aside from all my extracurricular activities, I was given a chance to go back to my junior high school and talk about my past. Speaking with those kids really gave me a sense of maturity. To think I would be asked to speak at the very junior high school that I was kicked out of really emphasized to me how much I had really changed. Life really came full circle. When leaving from my day of giving back to the community, I told the students that I would be attending Tuskegee University in the fall.

In April of my senior year, we attended a college tour of Historically Black Colleges. We visited schools in D.C., Maryland, Virginia, North Carolina, South Carolina, and Georgia. After the tour, my room deposit was due to Tuskegee. I was all set to send it when I got back home until we arrived on the campus of Morris Brown College. I remember sitting there talking to a student named Zack (who is now a friend of mine), and he was explaining the college to the family and me like - very intimate setting that helped to set this institution apart. I had a chance to see firsthand the camaraderie the students displayed, and during the short time I sat on that campus, I fell in love with it. But as you know by now, I am not a man to fall head over heels in love and disregard the facts at hand. When asked about the status of the fiscal issues the school faced, I was assured that the debt problem was being taken care of and the future of Morris Brown was not in jeopardy. That was put to rest, and the idea that I would have the luxury of being in daily company of some of the most beautiful sisters in the world switched my whole frame of mind, and the decision was made. Morris Brown College would be where I was going to school.

In May of 1993, I was released from probation, a luxury I had not enjoyed since the age of thirteen. All I could think was whether or not I was going to do something to mess this up. With High School graduation getting close, I put all my time and effort into graduating, and my entire focus was on making sure I was tight in all my classes.

I made it to the prom, but not without a slight hiccup. My friend Joel, our dates, and I had rented a limo for the prom. Everything was cool on the way there. I had some wine in the limo and was drinking on the way to the prom. When we arrived, we went in and took pictures and danced a little. After about an hour, we were ready to leave. Joel went to get the limo, but when thirty minutes had passed, I went outside to find him, and that was when I saw my date's father in the parking lot. All of our parents were there to pick us up. It turns out the limo driver left us at the prom because we had alcohol inside the limo. To my surprise, our parents were more upset with the people at the limousine company than with me. As we were all under the age of twenty-one, the limo company was supposed to make sure everyone signed a contract agreeing that we understood that alcohol was not allowed in the limo. We were not given any such contract.

That situation was handled pretty smoothly, but I was also cautious to stay out of any other potential trouble.

Next came graduation. I can remember that day vividly. Vallejo is a fairly small city and has all the attributes of such. People steadily in your business being one of the more pronounced ones. A lot of people were surprised that I was graduating, not that I could really blame them. Most of them thought I was going to be locked up by this time, and if I had not had that glimpse of another life, I would have proven their thoughts correctly. But instead, I was a free man about to walk across a stage, and I was in the local newspaper not for stealing cars or being arrested but for an article I had written concerning the trouble I had been in during my high school years. Funny how the very wrong I used to do, gave me a story to tell and a platform to tell it from. Not to be confused with bragging about being a troublemaker, I always believed in being honest about my past, which tugged on my teacher, and she chose my essay among a few others to be included.

Some people, like my old peers, were mad at what I put in my essay, but I only wrote what was true. This essay shocked lots of people who knew me. It didn't shock me because I knew I wasn't a slouch. I just never really applied myself.

When graduation was over with I still had another major issue. I had to make it through the summer, so I could get on a plane to Atlanta. I had not made it through a summer without being incarcerated since the ninth-grade year. This task was not going to be easy.

That summer, I mostly just shot dice during the day and visited friends at night. That was a habit that I just wasn't ready to break. However, I still managed to stay away from selling dope up to this point. It was hard not to grind, as all my partners were starting to make a lot of money selling dope. Even the ones who got locked up during the sweep were back out, back at it, and doing very well. They were the ones who were really stacking by now.

I guess my vision was more important than money because I stuck to my guns and didn't grind. A couple of days before I left for Atlanta, I went to spend some time in Sacramento with my friends Tremaine, Ray (whom we called C.C.), and Mike. We stayed drunk for three days, and then it was time for me to get back to Vallejo so that I could finish packing. When I got back to Vallejo, I was leaving for Atlanta the next day and could feel that the longest part of this journey was over, and I had made it with only one more day to go.

At the time, my mother didn't have a car, so naturally, I got a ride to the airport with PG. My mother and a couple of alumni and mentors (Kevin Matthews and Leron Patton) from the boys and girls club rode with us to the airport. My friends Valeka, Erica, Manel, Makeda, my cousin Treva and my Uncle Corey were also at the airport.

I was running so late that I had to go straight to the gate, and I really couldn't say bye to everyone like I wanted to. When I boarded the plane, I just kept thinking that I was really on my way to a whole new world. The flight attendant came up to me and gave me my jacket that I had forgotten. There I was on my way to Atlanta, GA, with only eighty dollars in my pocket. I knew a couple of people out there from Vallejo, but in reality, I didn't know what to expect when I got to Atlanta. When the plane took off, it hit me that I was really leaving one world for another. It hit me so hard that I started crying. I don't really know what prompted the tears, but for some reason, I couldn't stop. Maybe because I knew I was leaving my son and daughter for many years, or maybe because I was worried about being that far away from home. Thinking of it now, I wonder if it was the realization that I had made it through a leg of the passage I had not initially set out to successfully navigate using this route. Heading for a destination with goals in tow that I did not conceive possible for me, but someone else did and showed me what my life could become. Whatever the reason, I had to quickly get comfortable with the reality that I had left my comfort zone in California.

Chapter 8: Morris Brown College

When I landed in Atlanta, my uncle's old roommate Gerald came to pick me up from the airport. It was a hundred degrees and very humid, so as soon as I walked outside, I began to sweat. This was August of 1993, and I don't think the city of Atlanta or Morris Brown College was really ready for me.

Gerald took me straight to his house because I didn't have to check into the dorms until the next day. The first place we went after I changed clothes was the mall. I was so hyped I bought a $40 jacket on a whim, leaving me with only half of what I traveled to Atlanta with to my name. Here I was, over 2000 miles from home and only $40 in my pocket; that was a stupid move. On the way back to Gerald's place, all I could do was stress off all of the money I didn't have. But the money was already gone, and there was nothing I could do about it now.

Later that night, when he went to work, I saw a book on his desk entitled *Monster* by Sanyika Shakur. This book was an autobiography of an L.A. gang member, and from the moment I picked it up, I sat in that same place and read it cover to cover. There was something about that book that held my attention, and that was the first time in my life that I had read an entire book in one day. Not even in juvenile hall did I read any of the books that fast. "Monster" to me was more than just a good read; it inspired me to think about one day telling my own story to the world, especially the youth, not because I wanted to gloat about the trouble I got into, but really because I know deep down how many young boys are and will endure the same struggles I did. Without a fork in the road moment offering them another way in life or proof that there is another lifestyle that will pull from them who they really are, how will they make it beyond the confines of the mental prisons that poverty and lack of exposure often create? I want them to know they have a real chance in life to become the greatness they are ironically afraid of discovering.

When I arrived on the campus of Morris Brown College, all the memories from my initial time on this campus came flooding back. But this time was different. This was now my school, and I was part of a group of students who were all vying to get from freshman year to senior year with a degree to prove for the time and money spent. I looked at the women, and they were among the most beautiful I had ever seen. Intelligent sisters, here for the same reason I was, to get an education. At this point, I was ready for anything. I arrived in my room and was the first one there. I threw my clothes on one side of the bed and headed outside to meet people. The only thing on my mind was, I am not going to hang around any suckas. There were so many activities during our freshman week, which gave us a chance to become fast acquaintances with people quite easily. I became friends with a few people from our first week who, to this day, I am still close with.

One thing I noticed quickly was that a lot of people came to school pretending to be somebody they were not, and if I cannot trust you to be yourself, then I cannot trust you, period. A lot of freshmen were trying to sell weed and trying to smoke weed for the first time. I think everybody was just trying to establish a name for themselves with a certain reputation connected to it. One thing they don't tell you is that everything that goes on in the streets also goes on in college. People carry guns, fight and bring their ghetto mentalities to school with them as well. It's not that hard to get into college, but staying there is a different issue. I have seen many people come and go during my college experience, and strong-minded individuals with established goals stay focused and make it through.

Freshman week was cool. There were lots of social events on campus, a few at venues in the downtown core as well as at the neighboring schools in the Atlanta University Center (AUC). That was the beauty of it all. You had so much taking place between Clark Atlanta University (CAU), Morehouse, Spelman (an all-women's college), and Morris Brown College (MBC) campuses that there was always something to do. Morris Brown had a packed schedule of events ranging from orientation meetings at Hickman Center to socials on Founders Plaza and in front of the Towers. It was at Hickman Center during Freshman week that I met Joseph Milton (a.k.a Joe) from Pontiac, Michigan. We clicked instantly, and to this day, we are still tight. Our hometowns may have been in very distant states, but we had very similar backgrounds and a lot of the same interests. We had the same taste in women, liked the same kind of clothes, and, most importantly, we had the same ethics when it came to friendship. He had my back, and I had his. Whatever it was that I needed, if he had it, he would give it to me and vice versa. To this day, our friendship remains solid.

During all the partying and hanging out, I tried my best to be the perfect student at Morris Brown, but it didn't even take me a whole week to get into my first fight.Joe and I were walking, and this big dude was showing off for these girls and made a smart comment to Joe. We couldn't let that ride, so I went over there and started a fight with him. He just kept talking, so I hit him twice before he decided to fight back. By that time, we had a big crowd, and somebody decided to break us up.

So many things happened because of that fight. All the people that were out there started telling others that I was not somebody to be messed with. Even with my popularity growing, all that I could think of was how thankful I was that I didn't get caught. I could not have dealt with the embarrassment of being kicked out of college and living the rest of my life knowing that I was given the opportunity to attend college, and even in a new arena, I blew it because of the demons of my past.

One problem we all had was that we came to school with the same mentalities that we had at home. At the time, it was four of us that kicked it tight. My partner Joe, his roommate Smooth from Evanston, Illinois, my partner D-Walk (short for Deshawn Walker), who was a straight hustler from Akron, Ohio – always down for whatever, and of course myself.All of us clicked straight out the gate.

It was evident that it was not a matter of whether our academic strengths would allow us to make it through school but whether or not the wheels of our thought processes could maneuver the change required to turn the corner on our thinking and engage in the world differently. After eighteen years of framing our thoughts and mentalities within the confines of what we know as our "normal," changing all of what you learned and thought life to be was not going to be an easy task. Moreover, these would be the lessons a textbook couldn't teach you but desire would.

One night Joe, Smooth, D-Walk, and I went to Lenox Mall, which had to be a staple for all AUC students back then. It wasn't just a place to shop or one of the many places to grab a decent meal to eat off campus, but it was also more or less a meeting ground for AUC students. As we were heading down the escalator by the food court, two guys were heading up and giving Joe this crazy look. Naturally, Joe asked him what he was looking at, and instead of continuing on about his business, he decided to come back down the escalator. Sensing what was about to unfold, I stole on him before he got to the bottom. From there, it grew, and chairs and punches started being thrown. There were too many of us, and so, of course, we came out on top. Security and the police broke up the fight, and Joe, Smooth, and I were taken to county where we spent the night. D-Walk got away.

At first thought, this was like initially watching your life going backward in slow motion, then quickly accelerating. Here I was in a different city and state, at 18 years old, and once again locked up. The location was different, but the script for me was all too familiar. What I did not stop to think about before the first blow was would my future have been worth it? Would a degree and a job and a life I never dreamed could one day be mine be worth the wrong look from a guy on the escalator? To say I struggled with exiting my former thoughts and mindset that brought trouble into my life often is to give a false impression that I actively wanted to do better. Did my past ever teach me how to process differences and disagreements without using a fist or pistol? Was it so engrained in my psyche that if someone was to even so much as disrespect me by trying to question who I was verbally or non-verbally, my ticket to ultimate respect rested on who could win the fight? Sometimes I wondered if this dated back to the lessons my uncle taught to never back down, always face your opposition, and the least of which was not to appear wimpish - which on the front porch or in the park ranged from a look, to a threat or anywhere in between. Had that guy looked at Joe, and we ignored him, would who we were as men be devalued if we kept on about our business and not demand what his actions should have been? The complexities in college life were lining up to be quite challenging for those who knew no other reality. One thing was for sure, our degrees would be worthless if our life skills were not balanced. We vowed to avoid all fights that we could and calmed down drastically by being focused on why we were all really here.

Even though I hooked up with some cool folks and had some good times, I was really depressed. My routine after class was to study and then go drink two forty ounces. My grades were good, and I was having fun, but something was missing. I was always broke, and I was missing my now two-year-old daughter and home a great deal. Something that not even having full access to a car could fulfill.

The semester was passing by at a rapid speed, and while I was getting close to a few more people, Gerald was instrumental in showing me the 'keys to success' to some degree on how to have a successful academic year. He tutored me, and he also helped me learn how to balance my time between fun and schoolwork. It was Gerald who introduced me to Marcelino and Jeff (who we call J-week), who also became part of my circle. They were from San Francisco as well, so we had a lot in common.

Another person who looked out for me was Kurt, who had also been one of Corey's roommates. In every aspect, Kurt had my back. Anything I needed, he would make sure that I had it. He was there financially, and he would also break a lot of stuff down to me, especially what circles to stay away from if I wanted to be successful in college. At some times, he was the conscious guide making sure I kept the authentic separated from the 'room fillers.' Who really has your back? He would always ask. In college, especially Freshman year, it's easier than we may think to get wrapped up in the appearance of situations or people and not take two steps back to really evaluate what's going on around you. These are some of the most exciting years of your life if you live them well, and when my perspective would stray, he was there to bring me right back to reality. Back then, cell phones were not as accessible for my income bracket – (a student with really no steady income), but he took care of me like a brother and made sure I had one and knew he was only a call away. He showed all of this love just because I was Corey's nephew.

Black college life was unlike anything I could have expected. Out of all the good that came with this new world, we also had to endure prejudices. Ironically, these prejudices came from our own people. Morris Brown is located in the Atlanta University Center along with neighboring schools Spelman College, Morehouse College, and Clark Atlanta University. The common thread being that they are all (Historically Black Colleges and Universities (HBCUs), and like other predominantly black institutions, they were opened during a time when being an educated black man and woman was not an extended invitation to all but a 'by invitation' letter received by some. Even as such, we still had problems between us.

I can only give you my perspective on what occurs between these institutions based on my college experiences and the voices who gave this a place on the platform of truth by repeating sentiments from their respective schools. When college students believe and function as if they are superior to the rest of their peers in the AUC, you have to ponder where does it come from, how did you just arrive and feel so accomplished? Are we not all vying to achieve the same goal by way of different academic dreams? I often think of something I heard during my own Freshman Orientation, "Look to your left and to your right; not everyone who starts with you will finish," and it was true. I was confident I would, not arrogant, that I was better or less than the next person who arrived here by way of another course, at another school, pursuing another degree. To some extent, it reminded me of family dynamics: belonging to the same family tree, but the branches separate the have's from the have not's; the classist mentality breeding thoughts of I'm better than you because my last name is____, my hue is a different shade and my hair softer to the touch, my father does____, I attend____, and I have been afforded a lifestyle that far exceeds your limited experiences to date. That kind of attitude towards fellow peers is unbelievable. During freshman week, they are not just reminded of the golden opportunity they have earned, in some cases bought, but it is instilled in their thought process that their institutions make them superior to students attending other institutions in the AUC. There is nothing wrong with school pride; however, it becomes the breeding ground for ignorance to some degree and keeps eyes closed to the rich history that historically black colleges and universities have written. We do come from varying socio-economic and academic backgrounds, and that has and always will be the case. But wouldn't one think that there would be greater camaraderie amongst the schools realizing that the ultimate goal is to educate the next generation, network as we are evolving into our full selves, grow our communities and continue to build legacies beyond our now? There was a point in time when these were the only institutions that would educate us; the gift of choice did not exist, and if it did, it was not so readily accessible. We knew then, like I wish we remember now, that we really are not in a competition amongst ourselves but on a course to grow into our full potential. We're all black people, and that's the bottom line. We all came to the AUC for an education. We all are already believed to be two steps behind, regardless of the privileges life has allowed us to enjoy. How much more would we achieve collectively if we explored being our brothers' and sisters' keepers regardless of institution, where you were raised, your background, and your last name? How much more would we grow personally if we widened our nets and expanded our judgmental view of a person we do not know beyond the perception we think we have of them, which was gathered from a once-look-over?

I don't know the background of each student, but where I am from, black people fight for crumbs. It is no different in an educational environment. We're all fighting for the same crumbs. If one group has more influence than the other, it should be shared so that we all can advance.

Toward the end of the semester, Joe had hooked up with this brother by the name of Luke. As time passed, he eventually became a part of our circle. My group of friends was cool, and I was doing very well in school – actually, I was excelling more than I ever had. Despite all of this, I still wasn't feeling right. By now, I had figured out what it was. I was broke. Being broke in Atlanta just wasn't going to work. Over the holiday break, I went home and earned a little money to help survive part of the next semester in Atlanta.

With the little bit of money I had made over the break, I was ready to buy a bucket (cheap old car). I saw this dude with a Buick LeSabre like the one my partner Big Dre would let me drive in Atlanta. This car had a *for sale* sign in the window, and I wanted to buy it. I exchanged information with him, and he called me that night to bring me the car. The whole time I had a funny feeling because he called me at night. Joe and Luke had told me to wait until the following day and make sure it was during the daytime. As I am incredibly stubborn, I went against their advice, but my gut instinct wasn't too sold on the nighttime arrangement either. I muted all the voices warning against this idea and still went and met the dude outside their dorm. That's how bad I wanted my own car.

When he pulled up, we went for a test drive. I had Joe sit directly behind him on the passenger side so that he would think we had something. After I test-drove the car, we negotiated a price. When we got to the dorm, he kept trying to get me to take him home in the car, but I already decided that Luke would drop him off in his car. He didn't want to do it that way, so I got my money back and gave him his pink slip. When we walked outside, he pulled out a strap from the passenger side. I don't know what kind of gun it was, but he put it to my gut and took all my money. After that, he pulled off.

The entire time I was just thanking God that I had Joe sit behind me when I test-drove the car. There was no telling what he would've done had I been in the car with him by myself as he already had the gun on the passenger side, which was an indication that he had a plan. Once again, I had God on my side. I was just happy to be alive.

The next day I went out and bought hella shoes and some clothes. I was determined not to let that loss hurt me; even after all that, I still kept pushing through.

By this time, one of D-Walk's friends ended up being tight with all of us too. His name is Larry. Larry is the most country friend I have. This is mainly because he was the only one of us not from California, Ohio, or Michigan. Larry is straight from Louisville, Kentucky. He changed my view of people from the south because he was far from slow. Larry is the type of person that will go through hell with you.

By our Junior year in school, we had a crew called the First String Players. This title was well deserved and became somewhat profitable for us. We threw many parties and barbecues. Some we made profit from, and some we used for publicity. The String was all about having a good time and enjoying college life. We had the most fun at MBC, in my opinion.

This was another part of our college development. I feel if you are going to attend college, you should get the full experience. Not only was I making a name for myself socially, but academically as well. I went to many debates outside of Atlanta. I traveled to Washington D.C. several times, and I also went to Chicago, all in the name of Morris Brown College. Those trips were good for me. Competition allows me to show off my skills. I was also asked to join several honor societies and selected as one of the Who's Who Among Students in American Colleges and Universities. All of these opportunities and accolades allowed me to see that if I maximized my potential, I could really accomplish a great deal.

Even with all of my academic success, I still remained the same Shamann. I always had a good time and did not let my grades suffer. I can remember being in classes and hearing people make comments like, "How did he get an A when he's always partying." Regardless of my extracurricular activities, I excelled in school. I always knew my main reason for being there was to get my degree, and I was not going to leave without it.

My academic achievements also got me a scholarship from the Omega Boys Club in San Francisco, which was founded by an Omega man named Joseph Marshall and Jack Jaqua. With this scholarship, I was able to pay for school, housing, and meals.

Chapter 9: Omega Psi Phi Fraternity

The impact that the men of Omega Psi Phi Fraternity have had on my life up to this point is undeniable, and deciding to pursue a college degree changed the dynamics of that relationship significantly.

During freshman year, I had expressed my interest in becoming a member of Omega Psi Phi Fraternity to one of the Q's – (the name Omegas is referenced to often) on campus, and he tried to get me to run errands for him. That was a common error made by freshmen, but the mistake, in my opinion, wasn't in letting them know you were interested but in allowing yourself to get played before you were even eligible. I knew I couldn't pledge until my sophomore year, so I flipped him off and kept going.

In the spring of 1995, I met a guy named Dave, who introduced me to another Q on campus. After meeting him, he immediately introduced me to other people who were interested in the fraternity, and this became my new network, if you will, of people with a common interest striving towards the same goal. I was finishing my second year in college, which meant I could now pledge.

I did a couple of things for some of them Qs, and as trivial as it may have seemed, somehow, I was gratified that I was on their radar. Sophomore year ended, and I spent that entire summer trying to get ready to pledge in the Fall. I already knew the Greek Alphabet, so I spent hours studying the history and learning poems. Summer came to an end, and I felt ready. Little did I know that nothing I could do would prepare me for the next year of my college life.

As soon as school started, we began to *see* the Qs. There are many things I won't talk about, but my first night let me know that I was in for some hell. You can aspire to be among the chosen, hear the stories, read the pages of history, but nothing can truly prepare you to endure the intensity other than experiencing it first hand. To let go of this dream was never a thought of mine, and the other interested people were just as committed. Difficult times though, will not only build your perseverance but ironically has the unique ability to dissect your every word and test you on it. As the *heat* increased, it shocked me to see how quickly people started to lose interest. Initially, we all shared the same sentiments regarding not quitting, and I believed them. I kid you not; you had to want this, really want this, to stick with the plan. Quitting had always been a foreigner in my mind – didn't enter my thoughts as a child, a teenager, and sure as hell, I was not about to introduce this into my modus operandi as a grown man. So to say I understood how someone could come to that decision and be okay with it would be a stretch but to each his own. Brothers who were big and tall, short, average height, and medium build dropped line left and right. This had little to do with physical build and everything to do with mental and emotional vigor. It amazed me to see so many weak-spirited men. The group got smaller, even so, myself and others kept persevering.

I am honest enough to admit that pledging was difficult, but that difficulty would not compare to how much more painful it would have been for me to see others cross if I would've considered dropping. One thing that kept my ultimate goal in full view was the fact that struggle is temporary. It took discipline and focus to balance school, life, and the pressures of pledging, and while it may never be your fondest memories, the life and survival skills we sharpened during that time positively transcend into the bigger picture of life. Unfortunately, we did not cross in the Fall of 1995. We were disappointed, but we stayed focused on our ultimate goal. We had come too far. Invested too much time. We were going to see this through.

In the Spring of 1996, we officially became a line. This is where pledging took even more heart. All I could think about was crossing those burning sands into Omega Psi Phi. I can't say how many we started out with, but by the end of that school year, six of us became members of Omega Psi Phi Fraternity, Inc. through "Cold Blooded" Alpha Sigma Chapter.

We had sacrificed so much, but the adrenaline rush from finally crossing cannot be put into words. The campus abuzz with speculations as to when the probate show would be and who was on our line. People lined the streets waiting for hours to see us. The death march. Tributes to those who came before us and those who brought us into the fold. Hopping. Shot outs and the after party. The hits we got as our stripes. The brotherhood and camaraderie shared by thousands and hundreds of thousands across the globe. These snapshots into our new world made our sacrifices of wearing the same clothes every day, having no social life, missing Freaknic, and our entire school year seems so small. Even more irrelevant when you take into consideration that the four great men who started this organization in 1911 sacrificed much more and during a time when the social luxuries we are afforded today were nothing more than a dream.

To say that things escalated beyond my wildest thoughts after that night would be an understatement.

I was the Internal Vice President of the Student Government Association at school and a member of Omega Psi Phi Fraternity. I was having the time of my life. Even with the stars lining up perfectly for me, I still wasn't doing right by God and myself. Things went to another level of popularity after we crossed. We had many brothers expressing their interest in wanting to pledge. I don't know what it was, but in the minds of some people, we were stars. It probably had a lot to do with the love we had for each other and how we stuck together.

My fraternity was founded on principles that we exemplified well. Each year we tutored at elementary schools, held talent hunts for high school students, organized clothes drives, and spoke at various forums for children. Contrary to popular belief, my fraternity is not only about partying. Out of all six of my line brothers, five of us have college degrees, and a few of us have or are actively pursuing aspirations of post-graduate degrees.

In no way am I trying to convince you that we don't have a wild side. I can remember us being out at parties all night and stepping or simply being the party, but actions are often times met with consequences, and in school and fraternal organizations, this was no different. Our unruly behavior got one of my line brothers, and myself kicked out of S.G.A. This really didn't bother me at the time because it gave me more free time to study and have fun.

You would think by now that I had myself together, but something about these unfolding events convinced me that whoever we are as kids, teenagers, young adults, and college students, never really changed if we did not mature. So here I was in a different city, with the population of 4 colleges around me, bearing witness to the same mentality to some degree of high school students lacking guidance and, in some cases, a lack of self-respect with the expectation that I needed to be 'delivered' from my past and this was my ticket, added a little confusion to this mixed message. We were all lost. We were all on the road to discover who we really were, what we wanted, and who we wanted to become. We all more or less wanted more out of life, but to get there, we had to travel through the pool of mess to find out who we really were. My past was just a bit richer than others, so my wiggle room for mistakes would be a little riskier. Yet even in the errors that plagued my past, I saw it from a different perspective at times as I arrived at college well exposed to what life had to offer and the effects of certain risks.

Time to mature is right. As a result of my promiscuous lifestyle, I became a father to a beautiful baby girl at the age of sixteen and a son by the age of seventeen. Every day I struggle with using my own past to help them when making future decisions.

Chapter 10: First In The Family

Family means so many different things to us all. Framed mostly by our shared experiences, our brain separates our immediate family from distant relatives and all the sub-categories in between. For some, we define immediate family based solely on how the family tree lays out our bloodline; for others, we've compiled our own list of favorites picked from all over the genealogy map. In my mind, family was more than a title given to a group of people who happened to have drops of the same DNA traveling through their veins. Both a mix of the great times and the struggles create a wealthy memory bank that doesn't evaporate over time, forming bonds that can never be broken. Being able to rely on family members narrowed my immediate family down to a select few. My Uncle Corey, Auntie Let, my cousins Maya, Shack, and Monya, and, of course, my mother are people who I could count on and trust to be there in the blink of an eye. Grandma and Grandpa were instrumental in planting those seeds.

We were considered the outcasts of the entire family (at least, that was my feeling and experience growing up). Not only do prejudices of all sorts reign in society at large, but it also runs rampant in families where we're often divided by class and status. As we are the branch of the family who lived in the projects the longest and considered a far cry from being on the front cover of the next Forbes Magazine, we were treated accordingly.

Unlike those who are shamed by their past, I would not trade our up-by-the-bootstraps early beginnings for anything. Those 'stripes' taught us endurance and allowed me the unique opportunity to see life from so many different perspectives. I learned a lot about myself at an early age and developed a 'fight' for life which a comfortable lifestyle would not have been able to evoke so quickly. Amongst our cousins, I am the youngest, and I was babied in many ways. Nothing like the hardships that we experienced to whip that into correct order and teach this young boy the character strengths it would take to become a man.

When you have little, to begin with, you become less particular with your list of preferences. Call it a sense of gratitude; you simply cultivate the knack to be more thankful and less of a complainer. What good would complaining really do? I learned early that complaining does not qualify as a change agent and definitely not worth the energy.

I can remember growing up around roaches and having to go next door and up the street and around the corner to borrow sugar. The thing I hated most was that big block of cheese that the county used to give us. Trying to make a cheeseburger out of that seemed impossible; the cheese just wouldn't melt. I also remember going to the candy house. This was a project unit where you could buy candy, chips, and even chili nachos right out of someone's living space. They even had icy houses (people would freeze Kool-Aid and sell it out of their window in a plastic cup). Grocery stores were not that close, and we had plenty of liquor stores to visit, but candy houses saved us some travel time. We weren't depressed for not having the finer things in life. The experiences that came with poverty were natural because everyone around us was poor. Instead of basketball courts, we had milk crates with the bottom cut out for hoop baskets, right next to my Grandmothers unit. We played hoop with that crate for hours. All of our shopping, traveling, and movement was by bus in those days. My grandfather did have a station wagon, and he was the only one in the family with a car for a long time.

I often thought my future would be dulled by my past. That my humble beginnings and my zip code were more or less the plot points for how far my life would take me. Even members of my own family thought that we - the perceived less-than-fortunate ones, wouldn't amount to anything. That alone played a vital part in my transformation. That and the added fuel from the thought that I was always expected to be in some type of institution or dead by now. That is why it was never a surprise to me that people outside of immediate family thought I wouldn't amount to anything.

I have a lot of family who received university degrees, mostly second and third cousins, but no one in my immediate family. My mom attended college at San Jose State but did not have a chance to finish. My Uncle Corey was the first on the less-than-favored side of the family to go to college.

When Corey went off to school, that was major for our family and a time we all wished our grandparents had lived to see. Without them being able to bear witness, Corey still made it to college, and I was inspired by this. The Omega Boys Club in San Francisco paid for him to go to school, and we were grateful. Corey was in Cali one summer, and as he was leaving the Boys club, he was shot. Someone was on a rampage and then ran into the back of the car and shot Uncle Corey and his friends. This was a tragedy for the whole family, but luckily, he wasn't seriously injured. In spite of this, Corey still returned to school. After two and a half years in Atlanta and some amount of soul-searching, he decided to return home to San Francisco. Today, Corey is a successful advocate for children, a public school professional and speaks at juvenile halls, county jails, forums and conducts many workshops that play a critical role in saving our youth.

After Corey moved back home, I wanted to make sure I graduated from college. I felt that most of the family on this side was depending on me to end up with a degree. This became a reality on May 18th, 1998, when I received my Bachelor of Arts degree in Political Science from Morris Brown College,

[Graduating Cum Laude honors].

During my graduation celebration, I had the time of my life. Many people came from California to Atlanta to see me walk across that stage. This shocked me because I was never able to get them to visit me in Atlanta before now. My cousins Treva, Shack, my little cousin Johnta and my cousins Danelle and Suni also came (as well as a few other cousins). I also had my mother, my auntie Mary Lou (RIP), and my Auntie Dee-Dee. The thing that made me real happy was that Tremaine, Chuck, Joel, Quincey, Uncle Corey, Toriano, Cell, Gerald, Montoya, Valeka, Tina, and my friend Mario also made it. The icing on the cake was that my daughter and PG were there as well. I had over twenty people fly from California to attend my graduation. The arc had been formed. The dream was coming full circle. My one regret is that my son was not there as well.

This was probably the proudest moment in my life at that particular time. I was not only happy because it was my graduation and for what it symbolized, but as I looked around at my family of friends who loved me enough to make the sacrifice and travel that far distance, I thought of everything we had all gone through collectively and in our own respective life's. My degree was really our degree. A testament to how having friends and family around you who have your back makes all the difference. This day would not have been as exciting without this circle around me to celebrate it with. They had seen me through my worst and watched how the corner was turned, and I headed in a new direction. Was my walk across the stage, degree in tow, symbolic in some way of hope that they too may walk across their own stage – not limited to school graduation, but as it pertains to accomplishing dreams of their own. Whatever the reason, we lit Atlanta up that weekend!

Even after graduating from college, I was still hungry for much more out of life. There was a void that left me feeling quite unfulfilled to some degree, with degree. My life was still at a major crossroads, a place I found myself at quite often. I did well in school because I had something to look forward to, a goal I was striving towards - and that was graduation. Now, what was I going to do with myself without the pressures of college and the competition, which somehow kept my attention. What did I have to look forward to? I could not imagine living the transactional day-to-day of finding a job, turning up for work each day, and every two weeks receiving a check for the rest of my life. That routine would define my existence, and there was something about that scenario that made me restless. This was not enough for me, and the discomfort with the thought of just enough was making me miserable. There are still many things that I want to accomplish. For example, I knew all along I wanted to be an entertainer, but it wasn't until now that I realized how badly I wanted to pursue this. I had put that dream on the backburner so that I could attend college; now, it was time to become an active participant in the next phase of my life.

After graduation, I moved back to California and began working at the Omega Boys and Girls Club in Vallejo. I enjoyed working with the children and youth on a daily basis, trying to give back like PG. In ten short months, a great deal was accomplished. I was contacted to do an article with Emerge Magazine, followed by an interview with CBS for a program called "Save Our Streets." Another tremendous experience that came my way was being tapped to attend the inauguration of Anthony Williams, who at the time was the new mayor of Washington, D.C. As a Political Science major and one invested in the role of government, this opportunity was perfect. I am not sure how many people with my background experience all of these opportunities in a lifetime, much less over the span of only a few months, and I was thankful for the exposure I was being given, but I still wasn't satisfied with my life. The tug for more continued.

Joel, Chuck, and I began working on a rap album shortly after my graduation. Over the summer, we completed six songs and were on track to finish after Joel's graduation the following winter semester. I emotionally connected with the world of entertainment. To be on stage, telling your story or perspective of life with a background beat, and watching the audience involved brings about a certain emotion I cannot quite put into words. At the end of the day, isn't that what entertainers do? They tell a story that connects with an audience, which really emphasizes the power of the spoken word. People move to beats, but lyrics in a song or the poetry spoken in rap dives much deeper, and it's the words, call it lyrics, a testimony, life experiences, or dreams create emotional connectivity with the audience. What more powerful connection can one have in a stadium filled with thousands of strangers, all quickly becoming family because your story resonates so deeply with some experience they have had. I was a substitute teacher for a while, but my heart wanted mostly to be in the studio connecting the dots of our lives to a music sheet or standing before people spitting my life. In the beginning, we worked with an independent label by the name of Extra Records, which was owned by Chuck's Uncle E-Stew, and by the time our album came out, we were with Zoc Records, owned by Chuck and Joel.

Tremaine, Chuck, Quincey, Aaron, and I all went to Joel's graduation that December at New Mexico State to celebrate another one of us getting their college degree. We had a great time out there. Once we got back to Vallejo, I thought we were going to quickly finish our album, but instead, we hit a standstill.

After a few months had passed, I decided to move back to Atlanta to see what opportunities I could find. All I was taking with me was a notebook full of raps and the laptop that I am typing my book on at this moment (this was 1999). I don't know what my future holds, but I'm going to work at bringing my dreams to life.

Chapter 11: My Father

It has been said many times that the void felt by an absent father shows itself through a child's actions at some point in their life. I have debated that thought process for years, but as I traveled the journey from a young boy to a teenager and then on to manhood, I have had the chance to mentally chronicle the events of my life that either run parallel with memories of my father, or could be classified as void fillers.

Whether it was while celebrating major accomplishments or just moments we tout as minor achievements, my father's absence seemed more like the standard as out of everyone I knew, only a couple friends had fathers in their lives. Something that speaks volumes is that the few memories I do have of my father had in some way played themselves out in my behavior.

I have a semi-vivid memory of being around him between the ages of four and five. I can remember him selling drugs which afforded him the amenities of a lavish lifestyle furnished with a Mercedes Benz and women, too many to count. Those were the days when he used to pick me up and buy me anything that I wanted. Naturally, in a child's mind, that automatically made him my hero at this point in time. My mother, on the other hand, was often reluctant to let me go with him and would often refuse to let me go and spend time with him because of the danger she felt I would be in a while under his care. Her objection was at times met with anger, and I can remember the times when he became physical with her. To be honest, the hostility made me really nervous for my mother and scared at what the end result of each altercation would bring. One day when he came to pick me up, my mother would not open the door for him, so he broke the glass on the door to get into the apartment. Instances of this nature were never too alarming as, in my mind, we have been down this road often enough for me to have an idea, if it stayed on queue, as to how this would unfold. My father never gave me a reason to be personally afraid of him, as he had only given me two whippings my entire life. It was my mother, though, who usually caught the brunt of it.

During this time in my life, I spent a pretty good amount of time with my father, and my mother's gut instincts always rang true. I can remember my father doing cocaine with his girlfriends right in front of me and smoking weed, *the menu* dependent on who the chosen girlfriend of the hour was. These are images that don't fade with age, nor does the memory of watching your father get carried away in handcuffs right in front of you. I didn't then, nor do I now, understand why I had to see things that are inappropriate for a young child, but as I look back, it somehow may help me make sense of my own demons.

I remember meeting all his girlfriends as our father-son time was shared with the different women in his life. Where we ended up staying each night was on heavy rotation, and decided when we paid our visit to whomever was the girlfriend of the evening.

When I was four years old, I can remember us heading to Chicago, but there was one glitch: He didn't have permission from my mother. Even though I was legally kidnapped, I had a good time with my paternal grandparents and cousins. I don't actually remember how long I stayed in Chicago; the only thing that comes to mind from that trip was how much fun I was having. On the flip side and on the other side of the country, my mother in California did not share my enthusiasm about this trip. She asked him several times to bring me back to California. Since we had driven to Chicago, he wasn't going to quickly change his plans to bring me back at her request. My grandparents eventually put me on an airplane by myself, and I flew home. The summer that followed marks another set of moves for mom and I. She thought it in my best interest to temporarily send me to Pasadena to stay with family. When I got back to the Bay Area, our new address was now in Fremont, California, and it would be five and a half years later when I saw my father next.

Being with just my mother seemed normal. I had no idea that the right thing or the ideal family setting was to have a mother and a father in the house. That was never a reality for me. Through the years, I never thought twice about just having my mother around. I guess you don't think of these things until you have friends who have parents who are still married, society brings it to your attention, or you hear the stats and see the stories in the media. I probably missed out on having someone there to teach me how to treat a woman or how to take care of a family. All I saw men do was try to get over on women. Whether the woman was my mother or another female I was around, I never really saw a man treat a woman appropriately until PG came into my life.

I could honestly write an entire book on how instrumental PG (Pops) has been in bringing out an undeveloped part of who I was. All the life lessons accurately divided into the respective topics and sub-topics he guided me through. The lessons he taught me, not through lecturing or constantly pointing out my wrongs, but by walking the walk of a just man. His authenticity created a level of respect early in our relationship that allows me to truly value and trust his words as I have seen his actions. Unfortunately, I cannot say that I have always governed myself according to his examples, but I can say that he showed me right from wrong and the path that is there for me to take when I am ready.

Maybe I have been cruising through life all along and never stopped to realize the chunk of my life that I missed growing up without a father. While I do believe that children raised by two loving parents who are able to deposit and exhibit what it is to have a sound character, impeccable word, and respect across the board sets that child up to raise the bar of expectation on what is deemed acceptable by their own standard, I must ask, how different would my life had been if my father was consistently present? Does a man living out his own demons but present in his children's life create more harm or good? As valid a point as it is that the effects of a father's absence are often seen in his children's behavior and potential self-esteem concerns, I never wanted to use that as a crutch to excuse any of my behavior in an effort to justify it and make it okay. Perhaps, I did not miss my father as my mother's strength qualified her to be both. I may feel the full effects of his absence on me one day, but when my younger years come to mind now, I think of the dual role my mother played. Although she could never make me a man, she did a great job of being a mother and a father.

Chapter 12: Consequences Of Irresponsibility

One of my lowest points in life was the child-support factor. There was no denying it; I was a functioning depressant. Shortly after graduating from undergrad in 1998, my son's mom filed a judgment, and I started paying child support for my son. My daughter's mother also filed a few years later, which meant there was more money going out than coming in. I lost a lot of my joy during that time, caught in a transition between owning up to my responsibilities, trying to pursue my goals, student loan debt, and trying to somehow land on my feet. This is a tough road to navigate, and I remember quite vividly checking the balance on my bank account and finding out that my check was garnished before I could spend even a dime. As anyone who knows can tell you, when it comes to payments on child support, your bank account is fully accessible to collect the funds, no permission needed from the account holder or forewarning issued. To go to an ATM and see your account in the negative and you are employed, rips a part of you so deeply, leaving potholes of failure and frustration. Never before had I felt like such a spectator to my finances, and there was absolutely nothing I could do about it.

Without prayer, I would not have made it through that time. I wanted to do right by my children and take care of them. Here I was, a college graduate with a decent income, but every two weeks, I had very little and sometimes nothing to show for it. So it came in, it was taken away. If there was ever a time when your past came knocking, it was at your lowest, which for me was now. But I had come too far. I had too much to lose, and I was determined that I was going to eventually plant my feet firmly on solid ground soon again. I moved back in with my mom temporarily, and for me, that was a humbling moment. I had always prided myself on being independent, in charge of my own course for the most part, and here I was in my twenties, and this was not the life I had envisioned for myself. Though I was not locked up, the prison of my past ills was doing its best to take away my freedom. For a while, it won. I didn't have the desire to be the social person everyone had come to know. The pressures of life can drive you very quickly to isolation because enough negative self-talk can dim your hope if you don't let it out.

My friends, ST and Spud, were the only people with whom I truly shared the extent of my financial woes. Having a sound listening ear who gave different insight sometimes is the needed change agent to a situation that appears to be leading you nowhere quite quickly. From early on, Pops had always been an advocate for education and being resilient when pursuing goals. On my worst days, those are some of the things that kept me moving forward versus dwelling in the immediate with no vision of the future. My faith intensified, and God consistently made way for me to keep climbing the ladder of opportunity, which meant a great source of income. A (legal) way to earn enough money to pay child support, pay my bills, and still live. Even with a lot on my plate, I didn't want to postpone my dreams until a better day or time because, truthfully, people had endured more trying times than I was and still worked on their future while dealing with the mess of the present.

I applied to graduate school and was accepted into the MPA Program at San Francisco State University, where I enrolled as a full-time student, taking all evening classes so that I could still work a full-time job during the days. In January 2012, when I made my last payment and took into consideration that $30,000 was paid after current support, with back and current arrears being paid for both my children, I was thankful for how God designed me and all the experiences leading up to this test that had developed my resilience to not fail and never quit. As His Word promises, all things work together for the good of those who are called according to His purpose.

I can count on one hand how many friends while growing up had two parents in their lives. For us, it was mostly just our siblings (I have two sisters on the father's side that I do know- Brieana and Shashoni), our moms, and ourselves. Our family dynamics were configured a little differently, and extended family became the village that tried to keep us in line while our mothers and sometimes even grandparents were trying to make ends meet. Since then, and even now, when I share my message with our youth, I stress community. For the fathers, I encourage them to reach out to their kids and really connect with them and develop relationships built on open communication and honesty. Being an active parent, I have learned, takes both presence as well as dialogue. With the growing number of "fatherless" children, there is a call for all males in society to step in and be a father figure in the lives of children who may feel that void even more deeply than we perceive. So many fathers are absent, and so many of our kids are desperately seeking a filler for the void.

The dots of my life, though stretched fairly far apart, do connect. The son of a single mom with a colorful past meets the epitome of a man whose presence changes his chosen course and sets him on his way, not without first showing him a father's unconditional love. How could I not step in to help other youth when it was Pops (PG) who took me under his wing and fathered me as his own when in actuality, I was just a kid at the Boys & Girls Club? He set the bar so high not only by all that he did for me but for so many others that there's no way any child, the ones I fathered and others who I am able to support, will wonder who is in their corner or what a fathers love feels like.

My dreams for my kids are to find what they love, pursue it and never settle. There's also a reality side to dreams and a thin line a parent walks in being realistic with their children and not 'killing their dreams' while having an honest chat concerning their dreams. I never embarrass them regardless of my own feelings as to what they're in pursuit of, but during our one-on-one time, I do lay the cards out, and our healthy and honest discussions somehow usually find us on the same side of where they are and where it is they're trying to get to. Though you have dreams for your children, they also have their own, and our job as their parents is to support them however best we can. First, we need to be present to do so.

Chapter 13: Running The Race

I was always interested in government and politics and intrigued by the intricacies of how things work and the flow from government to communities. When I was younger, History was one of my favorite classes as it held my curiosity and provided an overflow of information. In Junior High, when I was not getting in trouble, teachers often told me that I should pursue politics. Those planted seeds, coupled with my genuine interest in somehow bringing about positive change in the lives of others, never left me, and looking back, my areas of interest needed an outlet and to be channeled. I didn't quite know it at the time, but the pull that kept me drawn to working in the non-profit arena was fueling me with the working knowledge at the core of how organizations function and why their existence is critical by being a recipient of their work.

I initially thought Law was the path I would take, as most politicians I had observed were attorneys. I started working for the city in 2008 while pursuing a Master's Degree, but I also had my focus on other goals, which I knew I would be pursuing as well. During this time, I met and became friends with a colleague by the name of Tracy Brown. She would always say, "you're going to run for office one day," and while I was excited that someone I barely knew with no working knowledge of my aspirations could so easily walk into my life and speak me into a position of interest excited me. Yet, as a firm believer in never letting people I barely know privy to certain details of my life until I'm confident that it's time, it was not until we became close friends that I shared my goals with her.

It was 2010, and I was on schedule to complete my graduate studies. At this crossroads, I thought a decision had to be made on where would be home. Do I still commute to San Francisco, or do I move to my birthplace, which shaped me and completely immerse myself into a place where I always wanted to be?

In October 2011, I moved back to San Francisco, and in March 2012, I was running for a seat on the San Francisco Board of Education. As I write this, I can remember the internal debate I had on whether I should wait, but there's something about the dire attention I believe our kids need that created and still does, a sense of urgency within me to show up in life as this is way bigger than me. So, my pondering was met with one question, "What are you waiting for?" People endorsed my drive, as the phone calls were pouring in with encouragement to join the race. Like everything else in life, there were also those who contributed to my drive by saying I was using this as a stepping stone to somewhere else, not knowing that I am a product of the system I work in. There's a difference between hearing of policies and trying to generate funds and awareness for something you've read about or a cause dear to you. When it's in your DNA, and you see yourself in the young faces of the less than fortunate or those lacking direction, your cause is much deeper, and your resolve to win for the children increases.

This made the campaign rivalry and the 'politics' of it all worth it for me. I had always been well-known in school and knew firsthand that being popular brings with it a rise in both friend and foe. Running for office exposed me to a level of patience and resilience I never knew I had at that level. If you ever want to find out quickly how people feel about you, run for office. Navigating through moments of being misquoted, lied on, and pictured out of alignment with who I really am, were reminders of how unintentionally personal experiences can become. These were not personal attacks against me, but in every race in life, when seen as a threat, opposition and circles will find it necessary to dilute your message and, most importantly, distract you. If you can't stand criticism and opposition in any race in life, therein lies a huge problem. Life is full of both, whether you are running for office or applying for a job. I stood my ground and set out to win this fight intelligently. My focus was on the district I would be representing, the families who would depend on me, and as I campaigned across San Francisco and through the neighborhoods, I connected with people from all cross-sections of life. Human exchange and the power of connection at this level was something I had never experienced to this degree, and seeing bits and pieces of my past in the lives of the people I had the opportunity to meet while campaigning somehow made my days of living in low-income housing and everything since come full circle.

June 2012 came, and my reality bone knew that winning at this point was going to be a straight uphill battle. Even though the election was months away and I had a lot of city support and endorsements from several democratic clubs, I had not yet received endorsements from any of the LGBTQ Clubs or the San Francisco Democratic Party, and when running against incumbents, you need those to really seal the deal. In life, like politics and any other mission I invest my time in, I remain a stern believer in the facts. With five full months before me, I knew anything could change and sway this in my favor, but regardless if it did or didn't, I am also a believer in maximizing opportunities and not quitting based on perceived losses. Here I had an enlarged platform to voice concerns and the strategies designed to address them, an arena rich with new connections and exposure to new experiences and opportunities that were further fine-tuning my perspective on life, politics, and myself. This was going to be a win-win regardless of what happened on that Tuesday night in November. To shrink into thoughts of defeat and 'quit' the race, if only emotionally, was to cheat a family who endorsed me and contributed to my campaign with words spoken, which time proved I did not mean, and to deny myself the chance to evolve. Didn't my past teach me the power of being an underdog is in the power of my thoughts? Each day following this internal dialogue, I set out with just as much determination as the first day and took from it all it had to teach.

On that Tuesday morning in November, I woke up with a sense of peace with whatever the day's results would bring. Admittedly I knew it was a long shot; reality already showed me that. But it's something about facing each day and circumstance from a posture of still having a chance in the game of life that did not dim my thoughts from thinking anything is possible. I've been shown time and time again that it is.

I didn't win in votes, but I still looked at it as a win. Here I was, the man who, as a child, many may have written off after three expulsions in junior high and time spent running the streets of California, speaking with parents on a campaign trail on how to best help their kids, tactics that may work and remembering times my mom reached out to Pops in the same way. Life had come full circle, and what was given to me when I could have very well been left to make whatever I so desired of my life, I was compelled to give to others and more. People knew my story yet dug deep into their pockets and donated to the campaign because they believed in and trusted the sincerity of my voice. My past was now my blessing as I was able to speak with people from all walks of life and understand firsthand their stories. I woke up on Wednesday morning a little disappointed but just as fueled to continue in my stride to make changes that benefit the kids. There was no downtime. The election reveals who won a title and seat at the table, but every day there is an election that happens in a child's life where they lose a seat at any table without the resources to make their way. This remains my focus to this day.

While campaigning the first go-round, I gained many new friends and forged new relationships and connections. I spent so much time on the road and in the company of like-minded people from different walks of life that these bonds quickly gelled, with the ultimate results being the focus. Just as much is to be learned and can be said about those we meet in a political arena who support a party and do not vote on the strategies noted on the platform.

When I officially announced that I would be running again in 2014, it was met with even greater support than my first run and endorsements from heavyweights who had a chance to meet me and get to know where I was coming from. Two plus years ago, we launched into the race with a mostly grassroots campaign strategy; this go-round, we have a campaign team, fundraising team, and consultants. Both approaches, I've found, contribute to a brilliant mind fed by the connection to the voters. This isn't just scripted campaign messages strung together, but a belief that regardless of our backgrounds, we are more similar than we are different, wanting the same things for ourselves and our families, equipped to be the change agents that produce the world we want to live in.

Chapter 14: Faith, Fear, And The Man

To establish a list of my fears and articulate them at any point has a greater potential of giving them room to breathe and come to pass. For ever since I can remember, fear wasn't something I really understood or even thought real. There were and still are things that concern me and occupy my thought process in terms of digging for a way to bring the best out of certain situations that have gone left. To some degree, I think my childhood taught me that. How to be fearless. Finding out who I was at a really young age eliminated any possibility of insecurities or me being taught who I was by society. Don't get me wrong. There were times, and still are, when I worry that an idea may not be successful or we may fall short in funding, but I don't fear the end result. My, at times, nonchalant behavior enables me to not become emotionally attached to an idea or result and quickly adapt to change and a new plan.

As I now look back and think on what crossed my mind while watching my kids grow up, definitely wanting them to enjoy high school and not follow in my footsteps and become teenage parents were at the top of that list. Having gone down that road, I knew personally how much it forces you to grow up prematurely and be faced with responsibilities that may not be handled at their best at an early age. I wanted them to be able to focus fully on school, have fun social lives, and eventually meet someone, fall in love, get married, and start a family. At the least, have the support of a co-parent who is as engaged in their role as needed and a partner in raising healthy children. Education, in my viewpoint, is such a game changer in life that I wanted them to be hungry to learn. Of course, that applies academically as well as in life. I would look at them as I still do and see so much achievement, yet so much more potential in them.

Watching my daughter graduate from high school and walk across the stage with her university degree was one of my most proud moments, as well as watching two of my sons (Malcolm and my stepson Damani) receive their high school diplomas. As a parent, you always hope that the best decisions for your child are the ones being acted upon, but then you let go of their hand time and time again, trusting that it will always be in their favor. The great thing about life is that you never really lose unless you quit, and that is a life lesson I continue to share with my children.

Raising a Black boy—in our country, especially at this time— brings about a different set of concerns when I think of my son. When he leaves home, or I know he is out with friends, I can't honestly say that it has never crossed my mind that he may experience violence, be caught in a case of mistaken identity, or simply just be in the wrong place at the wrong time. That is a lot for a parent to consider, and always rest easily. But again, if I fear that my son may become a statistic, what good does that do, and how much living does that take away from his life?

He has always believed in being self-sufficient, so it comes as no surprise that he is growing into an adult who is able to support himself financially, even if that means working two jobs at times. His integrity and character are qualities that could never be learned, yet it is his heart for God and family that illuminates from beneath his outer shell. As he works on developing his skillset to qualify for other industries, I know navigating the employment playing field at this time is not easy without a degree. What I have seen through my experiences is that school doesn't teach you passion; that's something you have to cultivate on your own. He's steps ahead where that's concerned. Regardless, one thing I've never done in life, nor will I do with my children, is quit on them. That I got from my mother.

My mom is a force to be reckoned with. In addition to raising me or trying to not have me ruin my life which I was on the road to doing very quickly, I saw her work with Headstart, Social Services, and as a Drug and Alcohol Counselor. Yet it's not her jobs that I most remember, but her fight to always be one step ahead where making decisions for me was concerned. She saw the traps of each area we called home and knew her son well enough to know where the temptation would be most intense and did what needed to be done to move at the drop of a pin. The older I got, the more she connected me with male role models as she somehow knew she could not truly make me into a man and only another man's influence would do that best. You could say she thought very differently than mothers of that time. She was cool enough for my friends to always come and hang out at our place, but was determined to make sure I was not a statistic. I think of the many sacrifices she made for me and the chances at a life she may have given up on or was never even privy to because I was her focus. I wonder at times if she looks at me and sees the fruits of her labor, that it was her unconditional love and her belief that I was a better boy than what I believed that has enabled me to become a better man than I could ever have been. She is proud of me, I know. But I do wonder if she credits herself as she ought to for the role she played. I wish she had the opportunity to travel the world with friends and be a homeowner in a comfortable neighborhood with people she loves close by. As a son who never saw his mother in a happy relationship where a man recognized her full value and treated her accordingly, my hope is that for everything she has and continues to give people (of herself and materially), karma rewards her kindly. One may think while reading this that I'm a "momma's boy," and if that means that I enjoy and appreciate the nurturing, sensitive side of a woman, then yes. When you watch someone you're close to change their entire life for you and make the hard choices for your benefit, and it is your mother, you can't help but want to somehow give back to her what she's given you. She brings new meaning to what it is to love unconditionally, and the day will come when she is the recipient of the seeds she has sown.

When I chose to pursue my bachelor's degree before getting involved in the rap game, that was evidence of a one foot in-one foot out mentality. The entertainment industry doesn't quite work that way. To thrive in it, you have to be willing to commit all of you, and education for me was first and foremost, and investing my talents for the benefit of our youth was something that I knew I would play a role in. My love for music made me want it to be a part of my life, but when an idea continuously costs you more than the income it's making you, some reevaluating needs to take place. Looking on, we can say it's the distance between the south and west coast, being late out the starting gate, or any other logical explanations on why our music career didn't take off as we had envisioned. But I've seen greater heights reached that were meant to be achieved with even greater obstacles. At the end of it all, what is meant to be is what prevails. Even then, our time in the industry was enough to show me how destructive that environment can be for friendships and, at times, people.

When I pray and ask God for His will and direction, I've seen Him respond in so many ways to provide clarity. He has been clear about what is and is not for me and which doors He has closed. Sometimes I think losses have been allowed to teach me humility, other times to expose me to something to be used at a later time, and some losses, quite frankly, are gains. When "we're awake," life happens with more clarity, as even when we don't understand certain things, we know it eventually comes full circle and is ultimately working for our good. If I could title the sermon of my life, that would probably be it. When I have been and find myself at my absolute worst, and things are falling apart around me, even then, things are working to my advantage. Maybe due to my active childhood and the things I've been exposed to, I don't lament over the whys of my world and invest time and energy to find the reason. I step into what's happening and move with the current. Where it leads me is often the answer.

I met 'Pops' and figured he was cool, but would be lying if I said I knew from our initial encounter the magnitude of the role he would play in my life. On my worst days, which inevitably meant they were some of my Mother's worst days as well, he was the one who would show up in the midst of my nonsense and stay until it or I was straightened out. Was I unknowingly testing him to see if he would eventually disappear, or was I simply being shown unconditional love and support by a man who stepped in the place of a father? Whatever the answer may be, he served as a mentor, a walking billboard on what it means to be a good husband, father, and Omega Man. I watched him with admiration on how he managed his responsibilities and how the real chase in his life was not material but instead, it was the things that really mattered, such as 'saving' our children and being kind towards people. It wasn't about his personal achievements but how he could use his influence to better a community.

When I think of who my hero is, Pops stands alone. I can't articulate how difficult it has been for me to process that the man who stood by me through thick and thin is unable to fully see the extent to which he affected change in my life and in the lives of so many. I have often wondered, do the greats ever know just how great they made the world by just being present and being themselves? What makes them great, I think, is that they were never searching for a platform of praise. Like Pops, they just know that doing what they can to make at least one other person's way easier is to have lived a good life. To be able to get a few to tap into their full potential is to fulfill their own purpose because they understand the power that lies in unborn potential and realize their gifts are not for themselves but to be used for the benefit of others. My prayer is that he somehow gets snapshots of the life he has enabled us to live and the dreams that came alive because he chose to walk in his mission and breathe life into it.

Becoming a member of Omega Psi Phi Fraternity Inc. was never debatable and thus has nothing to do with the influence the letters bring with it in terms of luring opportunities into your life, but more to do with a circle of influence I believe has and will continue to bring about great change in society. Of course, my hero being one of the first men who connected me to how an Omega man functions, opened my eyes to the organization I wanted to be a part of. Equally influential was the fact that being a member of the Omega Boys & Girls Club and experiencing how a group of men who support your dreams, even though they know you have nothing to offer as pay, can be the change agent that makes society, individuals, and a community that much better. Why wouldn't I want to become a member and continue the effect is the real question?

As an active member-both financially as well as involved in the work that is required, my commitment does not waiver. Not only do I remember how many others were called and few from the lot chosen, but in my roster of commitments, only the things I am serious about are things on my schedule. Don't be mistaken; I believe wholeheartedly in having fun, and the two do intermingle, but I won't commit to things that I'm not interested in because it may make me look better on paper. There is a cost to everything, and the price is often time and work.

This year makes it eighteen years since I've become an Omega, and there's nothing I would have changed from my experiences. I've met great men, fellowshipped with my frat brothers from all walks of life, and engaged in conversations too many to count that always gave me different perspectives. Along the way, I was awarded Omega Man Of The Year – Theta Pi Chapter, Omega Citizen of The Year – Pi Chi Chapter, and received 12th District Graduate Scholar recognition twice. Pops would be proud. I often think of him when at frat meetings or handling the business of Omega. The social aspect of fraternity life is unparalleled by any other experience, but the business of the organization is what he often emphasized cannot be forgotten in the mix. After years of leading in different capacities: the Northern California Area Representative responsible for working with nine chapters, Basileus of Theta Pi Chapter, 12th District Social Action Chair, and MSP Chair for Pi Chi Chapter, I have seen Omega through a different lens and had the pleasure of seeing the great effects of the work we do, both for members and our communities.

This may all paint a picture of me being rigid in my thoughts and all my work. Like Steve Jobs once said, "find what you love to do, and you'll never work a day in your life." That applies to all aspects of my life. It's a pretty full schedule of commitments but not draining. I believe that a requirement of life is to enjoy it for as long as we can, and so I do. Find me snowboarding during winter, at the Niners games during football season, movies throughout the year, and with my family of friends year round. Makes for a great life.

Chapter 15: What's Next?

The most frequently asked question when we get to any kind of conclusion in our lives is, what's next? We are really never in search of the end, but rather the continuation is what we search for. The next chapter. New beginnings. The answers to how and where we go from here. I really don't know what the Lord has in store for me, but I do recognize that he has enabled me to successfully pass through more phases in my few years than most people experience in a lifetime.

I am not proud, nor do I glorify many things that I have been involved with, nor do I choose to find a crutch upon which to cast the blame for my actions. From the mistakes I have made and the lessons I have learned to the contributions I made to the decaying of my community, I look back at those times saddened that instead of helping to move my race forward, I helped move the needle in the opposite direction. The selling of drugs, the fighting, endangering the lives of others through the use of firearms, and the impact that these actions have had on families who I don't even know, I take a step back to apologize for my then shallow thoughts, which left deep wounds.

I have had many opportunities to sit and give my purpose in this life careful consideration, and I keep coming back to one very crucial role: to relay the right messages to the youth right here at home in the United States of America. Home to the "I have a dream" speech, where the American Dream still seems out of reach for too many of our youth who are starting off steps behind. Ironically, equality, democracy, and freedom are three of our most touted messages, but so many are still enslaved, if not by a system, definitely mentally, trapped by the barriers which surround them. I feel it is up to young brothers such as myself to show our youth that mistakes in this life are inevitable and can be costly, but it is how we deal with them and the decisions that we make thereafter that determine where life leads us and how the next chapter will read. As sure as you are reading the words on this page, is as confident that I am that deterrents and traps are launched with a mission of their own which is to keep you from your purpose and those dreams you are hoping to accomplish. We must not allow our frustrations and anger to overrule what we know as simple common sense and the training that we receive. I've learned through ebbs and flows of my own that preparation enables us to have a proactive stance towards life while ill-preparedness drags us down the road of being reactive and steadily two steps behind the 8-ball.

It has been said often that we should not reinvent the wheel, nor do we have enough hours in this life for each person, adult or child, to repeat the mistakes of others and make many more of our own. If only we could invest a small amount of time in our youth and a willingness to share our skeletons as well as our successes, our children would perhaps be better equipped to deal with the pitfalls and the traps. Transparency shall save at least one life. To the child reading this book, I apologize that it has taken me so long to convey my story to you. If you remember nothing else that I've said, life is too short of digging yourself into and out of every hole that is too deep. Life can be a little unforgiving at times, and our past errs are not erasable. While I recognize that no one is perfect, think about the toll that each mistake will have on your life and your future. Is it worth the price?

At times I wonder what my life would have been like had I walked the straight and narrow path. True enough, I may not have been as well rounded as I am now, but is it really important to learn how to survive in the hood, or is it more important to learn how to survive in "life?" Surviving your starting point-where ever that may be is crucial, but surpassing that point by taking advantage of your opportunities is the real game changer. Surviving is not the goal; mastering life should be the plan.

If you are in the game, get out while you can. If you feel it is too late, then you've already given up on your untapped potential. I sit here before you knowing firsthand that it is not easy. For the longest time, I struggled with temptation, but being around youth and being able to have a positive impact on them daily, made me look forward to another day at work.

To all adults, both young and old, I challenge you to take the time to be a bridge builder. A few minutes a day spent with a child other than your own can turn into days and hours well spent. Let us not sit back and only talk about all the problems in our communities. We need to talk about answers and implement solutions because, as we know, any fool can recognize a problem, but only the strategic from the lot invest their time in working toward solutions.

I wake up each day curious about my future and what God has in store for me. There are times when I want to give up, but I have too much pride to allow a faint heart to hinder me from having my full potential realized. If I can go from a drug dealer, mental abuser, incarceration, and plain criminal to educated with a Master's Degree (a former President of the San Francisco Board of Education and member of the San Francisco Board of Supervisors), change is there for the taking. And available for anyone who wants it bad enough to be disciplined and committed to change. I don't claim to be perfect, and I know I haven't even come close to winning, but each day I get closer to accomplishing something big, and that's what keeps me looking forward to another day. Where will I be the next time you hear from me? Unfortunately, I cannot answer that question, but I do know you will hear from me again.

I started as a seed that was sown into my mother. Grew to be a water breaker and eventually a baby through the years and years of dealing with the reality of no father; what did I learn from that?

From a child to a teenager who has done most and definitely seen it all. From the streets to the parks, from selling dope to stealing cars, what did I learn from that?

From double jeopardy in the world of teenage pregnancy to taking what wasn't mine and maintaining a reputation, what did I learn from that?

From being in the system and having to walk straighter than the average. From being five steps behind because of my color and single-parent household. From dealing with family alcoholism to family crack addiction. From the jailhouse to the schoolhouse, from the schoolhouse to the world, from street life to college life, from college life to work life to depression. From not being able to be a provider, what did I learn from that?

From sitting here wondering where I could be had, I took different paths, from not recognizing and utilizing full potential that's why I speak to the person with plenty of time left, from seeing and repeating the cycles, from turning mistakes into lessons from having faith in God and never knowing the end result, and finally from the womb to the tomb; what have I learned?

Chapter 16: Pops/Pg

As I got ready to type the conclusion to this book, I thought about the chapters written, who helped fill the pages of my life thus far, and the man who walked with me through the very challenging years – by choice. What was it that he saw in me? And sadly, why was ill health allowed to take his memory and use of his motor skills from him? To question life on the whys of the less favorable moments is to give room to question the good, such as why was I blessed to cross paths with a man who somehow saw in me what was beyond imaginable to me and most others at the time. If only he could see the fruits of his labor and how far I had come because of him. I was born to a man who faded from my life but picked by a stranger to be one of his sons.

In a perfect world, he would have written the foreword, been mentioned in bold in the dedication, and would have helped me write the conclusion to these chapters. I gave a bit of thought on Thursday, June 12th, on how to appropriately end this book, and when one of the most significant people in my life took his last breath on that very day, I felt for sure he didn't leave me without sharing just one more powerful message with me.

Though dementia took his health away, he did not need his memory of who I was to take note of who I had become, as a way before I got here, he already saw this version of the present while others were focused on the stepping – at most times, the stumbling stones. He already wrote the chapters for the book while walking with me through the pages of time; he didn't need his own copy. He already knew who I would become, therefore knowing what his work had done. The planter sows the seed with a photo committed to the memory of what the harvest will bring. Many look at the soil, either giving up that the seed will ever sprout or believing it to have missed its season. The chosen planters focus not on time it will take, but on the fruit, it will bear. He was led to rescue me from myself and, in so doing, created a ripple effect that caused me to want to also rescue others with the unfiltered truth of who I really am and where I have been. Here it was that an outstanding citizen of the world would invest himself in another man's child to show him that he, too, can be a reflection of positivity regardless of his past. He never gave up on me, even when I never gave thought to becoming my better self.

Selfishly I still wish he was here. I wanted him to see what comes next, and next and in all the chapters thereafter, not just in my life but in the community that he helped save. As the tributes pour in, Pops, and you're being spoken of fondly by all as one of the greats, I wish you were here to hear how many, far and wide, have been changed by your presence. I think of you – who you really are and I am humbled to know that God chose you for me.

Pops, may my life achievements exceed the investment you deposited to get me here. Most importantly, will children grow up to be encouraged by the legacy of the man who stepped into my life against the current and turned it all around with a calm demeanor and fierce belief that neither I nor the hundred others you believed in would be a statistic. There was no plea from you to be acknowledged for your good deeds and no platform of arrogance announcing that you had arrived. You wanted for us all to go beyond our present place in the world-ironically a world that had given up on us, with one hand stretching back to help another and another helping another, and the cycle repeating itself continuously until we all "arrive." You wanted us to make it – and by that definition, you wanted us to be positioned as change agents in our communities and in our country. Your vision for life was always extending beyond your immediate environment and tapped into your innate ability to connect so deeply with the urgency of an infected umbilical cord; that gift time and time again saved a child's 'heartbeat.' As complex as we think that is, you taught us to simply be present. It's as simple as being present and available, and transparent. It requires an untainted desire to want the best for others regardless of color, socio-economic background, or active past. To simply believe in the good of others and connect to that thought, that in simply believing, change begins and continues.

May people come to know you not by what I say or by what they read about you but by how I live my life. How all of us in who you invested your time and efforts live our lives. That will be a price well paid for the gift of your time. I reread this mantra often and will continue to do so as I think of you: "You need to give a kid the possibility of success by giving them a success story they can put themselves into..." Thank you for being present with unconditional love and support. Thank you for being a dad to us all. Miss, you, pops!

Chapter 17: Second Run-School Board

To win in life is a matter of perspective, and I did not lose focus of my ultimate goals because my name didn't receive the most votes on a ballot. It caused me to dig even further in and gave an increase to a level of intensity that only being deeply connected to an end result can evoke. I 'woke up' and woke up to the reality that for me, there was no "campaign" to run – this is my life, and the fact is I have been running all along. Our life is a campaign of its own, and experiences serve as the training ground where we are able to look back at certain points and speak to the present with authenticity about what our own life has given us a deep understanding of. I want every child to be successful, and in so doing, I need for them to experience the opportunities to get them there. Through exposure, I know firsthand that it changes what we view as possible and how we color success. My goal is to help to broaden the views of our youth and for them to know beyond a shadow of a doubt that success is personally defined by the mark they want to make in society and that there truly are no limitations. I want them to know that to live and want to be anything other than who they really are is a waste of a life. Above all else, I want them to know that regardless of their starting point, any obstacle they may face, or their self-proclaimed shortcomings, they can live the life they want to as long as they are committed to the work needed to get them to that point.

With images of my past flashing before me, when I turn on the news or see media clips on social media, I can feel the dire need for mentors and leaders - for me to step in and help change the headlines. I can hear the message from my greatest inspiration, Pops, on repeat in my thoughts: "Education is the great equalizer that levels the playing fields." Not to limit 'Education' to a classroom setting only but to look at how our kids as individuals and pay attention to how they learn, what fuels their curiosity, and openly listen to what they express as their dreams and help them get there without smothering them with messages of who and what they need to be. The reality is every child will not want to go to University or work in the corporate world. Life is no cookie-cutter "one size fits all" landscape. But every child has a desire or need to discover who they are and paint a life they love and enjoy.

There is little separation between our time, our interests, and our personalities. How I spend my time is direct correlation with my interests which connects to my personality. I have always enjoyed speaking with people from all walks of life and different belief systems. So when out on the campaign trail, I don't struggle to make that connection or have what some may consider to be difficult conversations because of differences we may have. My life and my work is about building relationships, making connections, and the wealth that diversity (in thought and race) can bring. I've always remained true to myself – and in doing so, said no to things that were either not right for me or not presented at the right time. If something doesn't feel good, regardless of how great it may be, I know the cost of not taking heed to that internal alarm system flashing the warning light that something is not right for me at that specific time. I've learned to trust God more, and in so doing, I've learned to worry less. Be anxious for nothing, He wrote, and that in some way reminds me that this race (of life) is not to be run in a rush, but well paced and timed by a clock we don't control.

There is not a shadow of a doubt in my mind that I am exactly where I am supposed to be at this time in my life. God has blessed me with certain gifts and talents which are now being used for good and at a very critical time. I have found myself aligned with what I was meant to be doing, so it doesn't strike me as something out of the ordinary. With a maximum of about six hours of sleep each night, I get out of bed pumped for the day ahead.

Time between campaigns allowed me the opportunities to connect with new friends, even with people who did not support me the first time around. I became even more involved in different communities and was appointed to the Quality Teacher Education Act Oversight Committee. I had campaigned for over three years, which sharpened my skills in navigating this playing field. We have celebrated some major endorsements and worked through even more opportunities. My faith has helped to keep me grounded and far from the temptation to change my views in order to get votes. I have stayed true to my beliefs and remained resilient in the midst of mud-slinging. It's so easy to react when being disrespected, but it takes great focus and discipline to keep your focus on your ultimate goals.

Things have been much different this time around. I am working with a campaign consultant team who not only share my values – which are extremely important to me but have helped me to do things I was not necessarily comfortable with previously. Asking others for money is not something that comes naturally to me, as I am programmed to be self-sufficient. Therefore, picking up the phone or sending e-blasts asking for financial support was one of my least favorite things to do, but this is one of the campaign necessities. Money isn't everything, but in order to reach communities and communicate messages, financial support is needed.

When the story ends, and the message is written, let it be one that boldly scribes the legacy of a man who created a ripple effect in my life. A man who stood with me at my worst and walked with me all the way. He caught a glimpse of where I was going, and though he was called home mid-way, he had already made his mark. My platform and campaign in this lifetime is grounded in a God who saved me from myself and on the shoulders of a man who said life wouldn't happen without his son. This isn't about another accolade to achieve or title to claim. This is part of why I was born.

On Tuesday, November 4, 2014, I was elected to the San Francisco Board of Education (BOE) and eventually served as president of the BOE. Four years later on Tuesday, November 6, 2018, I was elected to the San Francisco Board of Supervisors. In between those two great runs, I married my long time love, Talmesha Hamilton, on Friday, August 4, 2017, and Damani and Dominic officially became my stepsons. On January 8, 2021, I was elected as the first Black man to serve as the President of the San Francisco Board of Supervisors. This book highlights my humble beginnings and trials and tribulations I have endured to become the person and man I am today. Stay tuned for a more complete and fuller story of family, elected life, and politics. Let's see what happens in my life's next chapters. The story continues.

One thing is for sure, your resume can change, as we have truly gone from juvenile hall to city hall!

Made in the USA
Middletown, DE
12 September 2023

38407766R00068